Lions and Tigers and Crocs, Oh My!

A *Pearls Before Swine* Treasury

by Stephan Pastis

Andrews McMeel
Publishing, LLC

Kansas City

Pearls Before Swine is distributed internationally by United Feature Syndicate.

Lions and Tigers and Crocs, Oh My! copyright © 2006 by Stephan Pastis. All rights reserved. Printed in China. No part of this book may be used or reproduced in any manner whatsoever without written permission except in the case of reprints in the context of reviews. For permission information, write Andrews McMeel Publishing, LLC, an Andrews McMeel Universal company, 4520 Main Street, Kansas City, Missouri 64111.

07 08 09 10 TEN 10 9 8 7 6 5 4 3

ISBN-13: 978-0-7407-6155-3
ISBN-10: 0-7407-6155-2

Library of Congress Control Number: 2006925241

Pearls Before Swine can be viewed on the Internet at
www.comics.com/comics/pearls.

These strips appeared in newspapers from July 14, 2003, to January 23, 2005.

Lions and Tigers and Crocs, Oh My!

Other *Pearls Before Swine* Collections

The Ratvolution Will Not Be Televised

Nighthogs

This Little Piggy Stayed Home

BLTs Taste So Darn Good

Treasury

Sgt. Piggy's Lonely Hearts Club Comic

For my fearless cousins,
Dean, Louis, and Vincent

INTRODUCTION

You might not know it by looking at them, but I spend forever writing and rewriting my strips. A typical daily strip on average probably takes about an hour and a half to write, and a Sunday strip can take twice that long. There are exceptions, of course. I've written some strips in under a couple minutes and, conversely, I've spent hours and hours coming up with nothing, but more or less, those are the averages. And all of this is before the drawing even begins. This of course raises the question, "What the hell's wrong with me?"

I mean, how can one person spend that much time writing something that's basically just a few sentences long?

I wish I knew.

All I know is that when it comes to writing my strips, I write them, rewrite them, rewrite them again, go back to the first version, go back to the second version, cross the whole thing out, uncross the whole thing out, and on and on and on until I look up at the clock and see that the whole morning has passed me by. And the end result? Well, see for yourself.

The scrawl to the right is just the first half of a typical eight-panel Sunday strip, the final version of which you can see on page 9. Contained in those scribbles, if you can believe it, is the layout of the strip (the boxes in the upper right corner), the delineation of each of the panels (look for the circled 1, 2, 3, and 4, not to be confused with the circled numbers indicating which croc is which), the characters that belong in each of the panels, the dialogue itself, and a few visual cues ("front croc—goggles, hat, no scarf"). In short, an unholy mess.

If I draw the strip immediately after I write it, I can decipher the

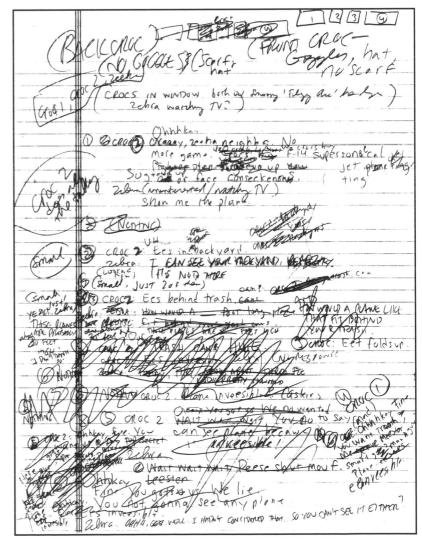

7

notes pretty easily. If I wait a week or two before drawing it, this cryptic hodgepodge becomes about as confusing to me as it is to you. I've lost many a good strip that way. Stolen forever by the God of Illegibility.

The notes (below) for the second half of the strip look much the same.

The interesting part is how many times I'll change the same stupid line. For example, the croc's line in the fifth panel was changed from "Nope, no siree," to just "No," to "Nope," to "No way, Bustah Brown," to "We no can see anyting" to the final wording, "No, we no can."

I also change the physical setup of the gag. For example, if you look at the notes on the top of the first page, the crocs were originally going to be having this conversation while looking into Zebra's window, and Zebra was going to be watching TV.

There's also a lot of dialogue that just didn't make it into the final strip, primarily due to space limitations. For example, in the third panel, when the croc says, "Ees behind trash can," Zebra originally asked, "How would a plane like that fit behind your trash?" and the croc replied, "Trash can HUGE!" Alternatively, he was gonna reply, "Eet fold up."

Similarly, when Zebra asks in the fifth panel, "So even if you wanted to fly it, you couldn't because you wouldn't be able to find it?" the croc originally replied, "Dat right. Finally, leetle lightbulb go on over you dumb hed." But after writing that, I realized that such a long line would never fit in the tiny sixth panel, and so it became, "Bingo!! We no can fly NUTHeeng!!"

But the most edited line of all is generally the final line of the strip, which is typically the punch line. I've written and rewritten a punch line twenty or thirty times, looking for just that right combination of words. I'll remove a word and put it back over and over, until I think the rhythm is just right. However, in this particular case, the editing was pretty light. I changed the final line only once. Originally, the croc that had just shouted whispers to the other croc, "You take eet from here." But I thought it'd be funnier if instead that same croc confidently proclaimed, "Me was debater een high school." And so that became the final line. I think the reason for the light editing here is that the real punch line in this particular strip is in the sixth panel, when the crocodile yells out, "We no can fly NUTHeeng!!" and inadvertently undermines their whole fraudulent scheme.

The end result of all this hoo-haw is the strip you see below. I have no idea whether people will find it funny or lame, because as of the day I'm writing this, it has not yet run in papers, and I could better predict the winner of the 2010 Super Bowl than I could the funniness factor of an unpublished *Pearls* strip.*

Why am I telling you all this?

Well, mostly because I ran out of things to say in my book introductions.

But also, because I want you to know the next time you look at one my weaker strips and say, "How long'd it take him to write *this* crap?" that the answer is this:

A very long time.

Stephan Pastis
September 2006

---

*For the record, I'm gonna say the Indianapolis Colts. And by the way, if any of you run to Vegas and make money off this tip, the ethical thing to do would be to send me half of it.

This entire series was done after the whole Jayson Blair incident occurred at the *New York Times*. Blair was a reporter accused of fraudulent reporting. After seeing the news accounts of Blair, I thought I'd have Rat turn in some fake stories. Rat and fraud go together like wine and cheese.

RAT, "THE NEW YORK TIMES" REPORTER

BAGHDAD - Today in Baghdad, this reporter was ushered into the underground bunker of deposed ruler Saddam Hussein.

Saddam, dressed only in boxer shorts and a pair of 'Birkenstocks,' sat quietly upon a bcanbag, playing his 'Gameboy' and occasionally weeping. A nearby stereo played what sounded like American country music. I asked the former tyrant what he was listening to.

"'Dixie Chicks,'" he muttered. "Nothing but 'Dixie Chicks.'"

Eventually, Saddam was in fact found underground, although I don't believe he was playing a Game Boy.

11

RAT, "THE NEW YORK TIMES" REPORTER

BAGHDAD -- Today in Baghdad, I found all of the weapons of mass destruction. They were hidden in a downtown convenience store.

The weapons were right behind the counter, just to the left of the adult magazines. I asked the store's clerks, Punjab and Abu, how it was that Hans Blix could have missed these.

"Well," said Punjab, "It looked like Blix was headed straight for them, when suddenly, he made a beeline for the girlie magazines."
"Yeah," added Abu, "That Blix is one lonely guy."

After this ran, some people felt compelled to tell me that Punjab was a city, not a person. I knew that, but used it here anyway because I thought it was a funny-sounding word.

I HEARD YOU QUIT YOUR JOB AT "THE NEW YORK TIMES."

YEAH...I WANTED MORE EXPOSURE, SO I GOT A JOB AT ONE OF THE SUPERMARKET TABLOIDS.

HOW IS IT GOING?

BAD...THEY HAVE ALL THESE STANDARDS...YOU HAVE TO GET THREE SOURCES TO VERIFY A STORY, AND YOU CAN'T MAKE UP ALL OF YOUR QUOTES, AND BLAH BLAH BLAH BLAH....

... I MISS "THE TIMES."

"...NATURE ABHORS A VACUUM."

WHAT'S IT THINK OF THE COFFEE MAKER?

HE NEVER ANSWERS MY QUESTIONS.

I kept having to turn Pig's back to the girl, or put some distance between the two of them, so it didn't look like the two of them were, uh, you know, "familiar." These are the things you worry about when you're a syndicated cartoonist.

Every time this Chiapas rebel appeared, he drew complaints from people telling me how wonderful the Chiapas rebels were and how wrong I was for showing them in a comical light. I suppose one should never be comical in the comics.

I used to make obscene gestures myself, until everyone started shooting each other.

Continuity is not always *Pearls'* greatest strength. Characters get jobs one day and then you never hear about it again. Lynn Johnston I am not.

This was supposed to be an entire series, but I couldn't think of any more funny strips, so I just let it sit on my shelf for a while. Months later, when I realized I was still stuck, I decided to just run it as a stand-alone Saturday strip.

For some reason, people who would never think of saying hello to their neighbor can establish a level of intimacy with a complete stranger in a chat room.

I believe this series first ran when *Pearls* was a Web-only strip in 2000 and 2001, but I did not bring it back to run in print until 2003. I think I was a little worried about the effect the "breast theme" would have on newspaper editors.

I'm proud of this strip, as I was able to slip "breast," "rack," "melon," and "jug" into the American comics page. Context is everything.

This series originally ended with a big, long Sunday strip. I decided after the fact that the strip was not funny enough to justify being a whole Sunday, so I shortened it considerably and turned it into this Saturday strip.

For those of you keeping score at home, I believe this strip holds the all-time *Pearls* record for most panels (twenty-two). On an unrelated note, that monkey joke rocks.

This strip was a big hit with readers. Originally, it said "#*$%ing," but using the last three letters like that too closely telegraphed a certain swear word, so I changed it. Using the word "#*$%ing" on the American comics page is a good way of not staying on the American comics page.

This whole joke depended upon one's ability to read the tiny words on the cup, which few newspaper readers could do because of how small comics are now printed in most papers. I have learned through exhaustive research that jokes are funnier when you can read them.

The question asked by Rat is an ancient Zen riddle that has puzzled philosophers for centuries. Little did they know the solution was this simple.

21

I am a big Cal Bears fan. Thus, the pennants in the panel with the pool table.

This was a popular strip. Looking back at it, though, I think it would have been funnier with an extra panel between the second and third panels, where Pig just looks down and says nothing. The pause would make you think he was taken aback by the news and about to say something sympathetic. Then the last line would have had more of a punch.

Pig is rather easy to write for. He just needs to misunderstand everything said to him, and then when it's explained to him, he needs to misunderstand that, too.

Apparently, everyone in the *Pearls* neighborhood has siding on their houses. Science has no explanation for this.

23

I'm a big Tiger Woods fan and have done a number of strips to try and get his attention. I think I'm secretly hoping that he'll invite me over for a beer. Sadly, it hasn't worked, and I have been forced to drink by myself.

Canadian bacon needs to be called Canadian baloney. It does not merit the "bacon" name.

Dear President Bush,
There are 192 countries. So far, you've only bombed two.

Even if you win re-election, you only have 65 months left in office.

8/17

If we are to get them all, you will need to bomb three per month from here on out.

For us to sustain that kind of pace, you will need to stop wasting time asking the U.N. and Congress for approval. They are silly girly-girls.

P.S. If we have extra time, I suggest hitting France more than once.

DON'T TELL ME YOU'RE GONNA SEND A LETTER LIKE THAT TO THE PRESIDENT OF THE UNITED STATES...THEY'RE GONNA INVESTIGATE YOU FOR BEING SUCH A WHACKO.

OKAY....OCTOBER IS MEXICO, CANADA AND HAWAII.

NO, NO, SIR, HAWAII'S OURS.

As we say in the business, "This one got letters." Predictably, half the readership was outraged and half the readership was laughing. One large paper in the Midwest was so upset that I had introduced a political topic into a normally apolitical comic strip that they took the rather unusual step of issuing an apology for the strip. The apology, which ran the same day as the strip, explained that they were not able to stop the comic from running because Sunday sections are printed far in advance by an outside party. They promised that their procedures would be changed so that in the future, comics such as this could be caught and removed before publication. Ironically, it was that apology—and not the strip—that drew a slew of angry letters the next week.

I think an unseen element (such as the crocs in the audience here) can be very funny. It lets people's imaginations run wild.

Most of the dead zebras listed in the second panel were named after employees at my syndicate. I don't think they found that amusing.

I have a cousin named Nicky. The dead zebras are always named after people I know.

Again, another funny unseen image. And besides, I couldn't draw a lion to save my life.

I'm fairly certain that the line, "My chickens have some subpoenas to serve," had never before been uttered on the American comics page.

If you're ever in need of comic strip material, throw in a monkey reference. They're gold.

I can't say the word "porn" on the comics page. So I have to say "adult entertainment." Oh, the sacrifices I make.

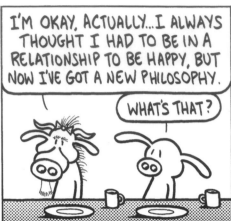

Pearls used to have a lot more puns than it has now. I try not to use them quite as much anymore.

I'm gonna give this animal the "Ugliest Character Ever to Appear in *Pearls* Award."

I don't think I've ever even watched a complete *Survivor* episode, but I know they do that at the end.

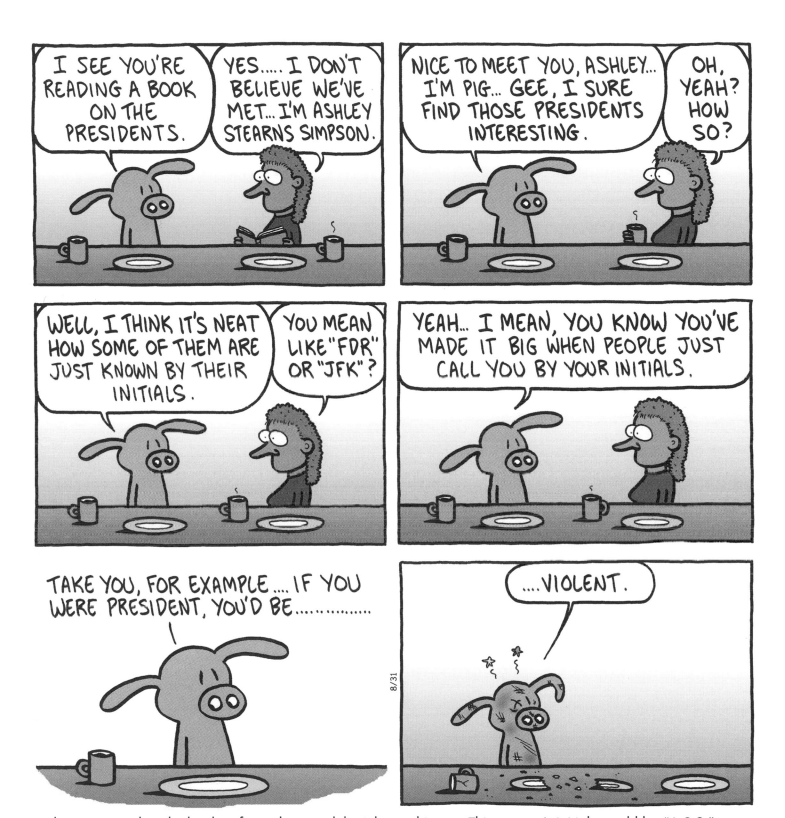

Rather surprisingly, I think a lot of people missed the joke on this one. This woman's initials would be "A.S.S."

31

All right, I've changed my mind. *This* is the winner of the "Ugliest Character Ever to Appear in *Pearls* Award."

More monkeys. Again, instant gold. If you can't make a monkey strip funny, you need to retire. It'd be like an NBA player not being able to dunk a Nerf ball through a Nerf hoop.

The funniest part about this strip is the guy who wrote to me to say that I got the Old English dialect wrong. He emphatically pointed out that the sentence "Howeth canneth that beith" was just not something they would have said (as though I might not have known that). Even funnier, he then went on to correct all of the other mistakes.

Between my love of anthropomorphizing and death, it was only natural that I eventually cover piggy banks, which are traditionally smashed to bits when filled.

Maybe it's just me, but the colder and harsher my strip gets, the more I laugh.

I never leave the toilet seat up because I never put it up in the first place.
(Kidding. Just kidding. Well . . . sort of.)

Any character who ever expresses unbridled optimism and faith in the goodness of mankind is always doomed in *Pearls*. This much I know.

For those who are curious, slipping "premenstrual syndrome" into the Sunday funnies can generate letters to the editor.

This was a popular little series, probably because Pig looks kind of cute in that helmet. I'm just proud of getting Sonny Bono mentioned in the same panel as Pope Pius IX.

Very bad pun.

Oh, man, an even worse pun. *Where was my editor?!*

The Legend of Orro by Rat

...The brothers Zorro and Orro stabbed the soldier.
...The soldier died.

Zorro made three quick slashes with his sword upon the wall, leaving his trademark "Z." Zorro hopped on his horse and fled.

Orro made three quick slashes with his sword upon the wall, but it looked nothing like an "O."

Frantically, Orro made more slashes, but it still looked nothing like an "O."

Orro turned his face to the heavens and screamed, "Why are O's so #&%@$*# hard?!?" A group of soldiers shot Orro in the back.
Orro died.

Approaching the scene, the soldiers quickly recognized the dreaded mark of Zorro, but were baffled by Orro's sad "O."

"Why did this man draw a triangle?" asked the first soldier.
"I think it's a star," said the second soldier.
"It is an illegible mess," declared the captain, "Shoot him again for bad penmanship."
They shot Orro again.

9/21

WE CAN'T ALL BE ZORRO.

People seemed to really like this one. I think somehow we can all relate to poor Orro.

Dear Dan Rather,
Everyone says you're a little nuts. Not me.
I think you're special...

....like Kenny, the kid down the block who got hit in the head by a brick.

P.S. I think you'd like Kenny.

Dear Ted Koppel,
Everyone says you wear a wig. Not me. I think it's a small, furry rodent.

I say this with some confidence because one night when you were doing a story on tobacco farming, a small pinkish hand poked out of your hair and waved hello.

P.S. Please give my regards.

After this ran, someone from Ted Koppel's *Nightline* office wrote to say that Ted loved the strip and would really like to have the original. I sent it to him.

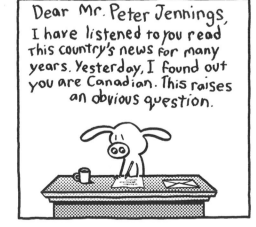

Dear Mr. Peter Jennings,
I have listened to you read This country's news for many years. Yesterday, I found out you are Canadian. This raises an obvious question.

Are you a spy?

P.S. Do not pat Mr. Koppel on the head.

I think Larry King is dressed by a posse of mean-spirited clowns. The colors, the weird suspenders, the goofy glasses, the hair . . . it all makes sense.

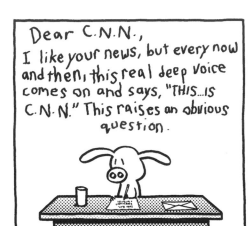

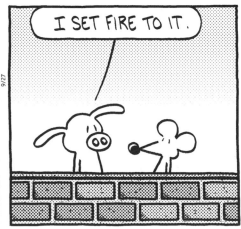

I'm willing to bet that the phrase "adult entertainment" has never been used in *Hagar the Horrible*.

I've had friends who've dated control freaks like this. Well, maybe not this bad, but close.

Poor Pig.

This is a nice little Hallmark card until that last death-filled panel. I believe Hallmark frowns on the "watching your friends be eaten" motif.

This series is one of those instances where if you just think up the concept, the jokes will write themselves.

By this day, I had grown quite tired of drawing aquariums.

This line comes from the movie *A Few Good Men*, which I've never seen. I'd see more movies, but other people are frequently in the audience. I hear that Elvis Presley often reserved entire movie theaters just so he could see movies without other people. For that reason alone, I consider him a genius.

Dear Comics Reader:

We here at "Pearls" feel that the format of Sunday strips is a waste of your time. Why should you, the reader, have to read through numerous panels of dialogue when all you really want is the punchline?

Thus, in order to maximize your comic enjoyment, we here at "Pearls" have taken the actual punchlines from four other popular strips and given those lines to your favorite "Pearls" characters.

No wasted panels. No boring set-up dialogue. Just pure comic pleasure. . . We hope you enjoy.

pearls

...Four Times the Humor, at One-Fourth the Price

All of these punch lines really did appear in these other strips on the date I mentioned, 10/20/02. However, when the company that produces the color for my Sunday strip got ahold of this, they inexplicably *changed* the date to "10/19/02." Thus, anyone who looked up those strips for 10/19/02 (and believe me, there were readers who did this) found no such punch lines on that date and thought I was a big, fat liar.

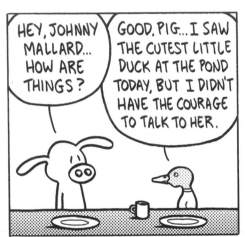  

Readers seemed to like this one. Its rather dark nature did produce some complaints, though.

After this appeared, some reader wrote to me and was like, "I still use 'said' and 'says,'" and I was like, "Whatever."

The minute I heard about what feng shui was, I knew it was tailor-made for abuse by Rat.

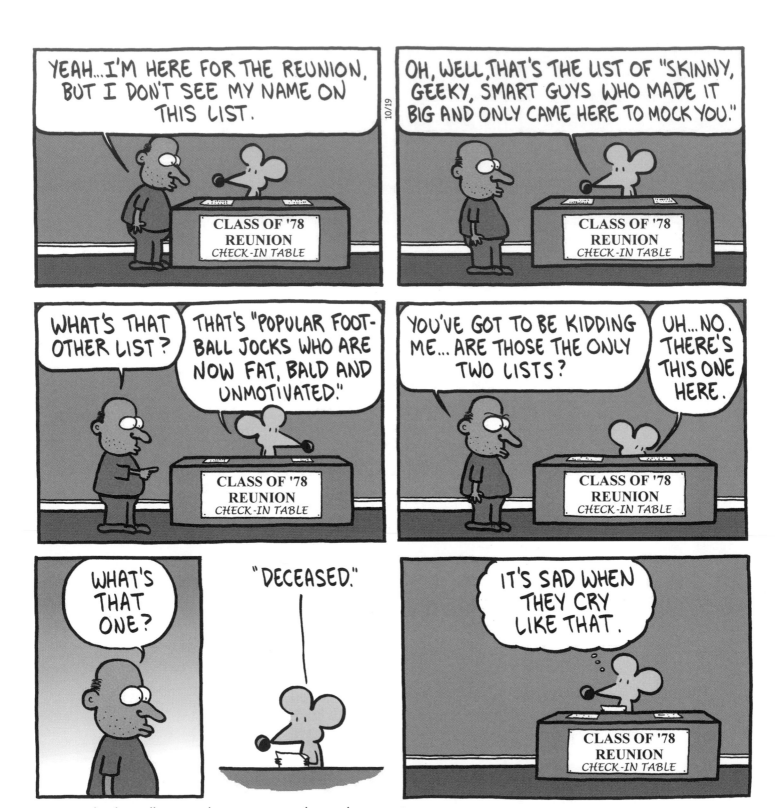

Does anybody really go to their reunion with good motives?

The Cubby series first appeared when *Pearls* was a Web-only comic back in 2001. I redrew the strips for newspapers in late 2003.

You won't see "stripper groping" mentioned in *Garfield*.

On the same day this strip was published, I was the guest artist for Scott Adams on *Dilbert*, meaning that I got to draw that day's *Dilbert* strip. What I drew that day was Dilbert dead in a coffin and Rat rejoicing that all of Scott's newspaper slots had opened up. Because *Dilbert* is published practically everywhere, I knew that a ton of people would be getting their first look at my type of humor that day and would then maybe take a glance at *Pearls* for the first time. What I didn't think of ahead of time was that anyone doing this would see a dead Dilbert at his funeral followed by a dead horny fly at *his* funeral, which is just a little too much death (even for me).

This strip reminds me of someone I used to work with who once called her son to say she had lost her cell phone and had searched all through her purse and couldn't find it anywhere. Her son then asked her what she was calling him on. She found her cell phone.

The first time I saw "dolphin-free" printed on a can of tuna, I knew it was a perfect strip for Pig.

This hostage series was originally scheduled for publication on an earlier date, but at the time, there was a prominent story about an American journalist who had been taken hostage in the Middle East. So the entire three-strip series was pulled and not published until over a year later.

Some people didn't understand this one. Pig hears the word "latter" as "ladder."

The Adventures of Detective Bob by Rat

Detective Bob received a telephone call from his old friend, Sherlock Holmes.

"I need your help," said Sherlock..."It's the case of the hooded bandit."

"Tell me more," said Bob.

"He wears a bedsheet over his head," said Sherlock..."We haven't a clue who he is."

"The solution is elementary, Sherlock. Simply examine the beds of all the townsfolk. The bed of the criminal will have a distinctive feature."

"A distinctive feature?" asked Sherlock... "What could that be?"

11/2

"No sheet, Sherlock."

I was absolutely shocked that I got away with this, and I still believe it's because most of the people that would normally complain (i.e. older people) were just not familiar with the expression "No sh*t, Sherlock." Had those people known that I had so closely telegraphed the word "sh*t" in the Sunday funnies, there would have been trouble.

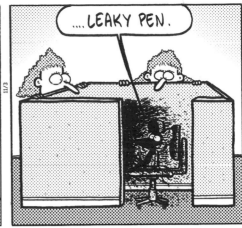

Not wanting to be outdone by my use of the word "sh*t" on Sunday, I introduced the topic of Internet porn on Monday.

I still have trouble remembering that most "negative" test results are actually a "positive" bit of news.

When I was a lawyer, someone at my firm got the bright idea to put an anonymous suggestion box in the kitchen area. At the time, there was another lawyer at my firm whose last name was Eberle. The two of us goofed on each other endlessly. Well, the minute I saw a suggestion box for anonymous notes, I made sure to stuff at least two notes a day in there that said, "I caught Eberle stealing office supplies."

60

Salzburg, Austria c. 1764

I'M SORRY, MR. MOZART, BUT YOUR KID'S JUST OUT OF HAND. FORTUNATELY, THEY MAKE SOME GREAT DRUGS NOW THAT CAN ELIMINATE ALL SIGNS OF A.D.D.

LET'S DO IT. I WANT THE BEST FOR MY LITTLE WOLFIE.

East St. Louis, Illinois c. 1934

LISTEN, MS. DAVIS... MILES JUST CAN'T SEEM TO FOCUS IN CLASS. BUT I CAN RECOMMEND A TERRIFIC DRUG THAT CAN MAKE HIM JUST LIKE THE OTHER KIDS.

OH, WHAT A WONDERFUL IDEA.

Liverpool, England c. 1950

...I'M TELLING YOU, MR. McCARTNEY, HE JUST SITS IN CLASS AND WHISTLES THESE SILLY LOVE SONGS.

OKAY, OKAY..... GIVE HIM THE DRUGS...I'D HATE FOR PAUL TO FALL BEHIND.

Pearls Before Swine c. 2003

This one drew a flood of angry e-mail, mostly from parents who had made the decision to put their child on some kind of drug for A.D.D. Predictably, it also drew a lot of praise from the antidrug faction. But what I really wanted to see was mail from irate fans of Pat Boone. Sadly, there was none.

This entire week was my tribute to my cartooning hero, Charles Schulz. Schulz probably influenced me more than any other cartoonist.

For the musical notes here, I just copied a section of notes that Schulz had drawn in one of his Schroeder strips (in fact, I think Snoopy's head was blocking a couple of the notes at the very end, so I had to wing those). But when it was published, people who know music must have then played it on their pianos, because they immediately wrote in to tell me exactly what the piece was. (For those of you who want to figure it out for yourself, I won't give it away.)

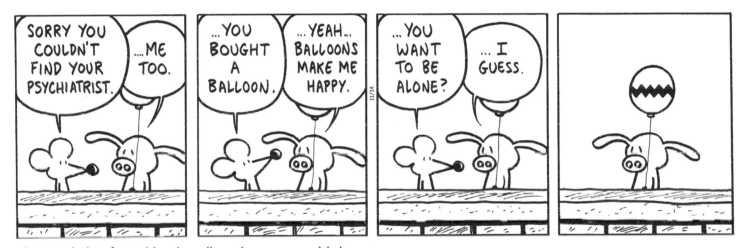

That's Schulz's famed brick wall, as best as I could draw it.

A couple years after this "Got Milk?" parody ran, I got an e-mail from the ad executive who had created this famous ad campaign, saying that he was a big fan of *Pearls*. Ironically, he had never seen the parody strip I'd done two years earlier. I mailed him a copy of the *Pearls* book that contained the strip and he in turn sent me a signed copy of his book containing all the "Got Milk?" photos.

This was one of the most popular series I've done so far. I guess a lot of people identified with Rat, or at least wanted to be able to say the things he said.

This one was far and away the most popular strip in the series.

Because the unofficial censorship code for American newspaper comics is stuck somewhere in the 1950s, you're generally not allowed to use the word "screwed" on the comics page. But without that word, this particular strip loses a lot, and so my syndicate let me do it.

66

This lost some people. The "C" and "H" Pig is referring to here are the "C" and "H" you see on your faucet handles (i.e. cold and hot).

This is another old series that first ran on the Web in 2001.

I believe this was the first depiction of a gay electric razor on the American comics page. I'm clearly a trailblazer.

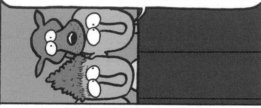

I absolutely cannot stand neighbors who let their dogs bark all day. It drives me insane. Rat is definitely me here.

After writing some of my strips, I sometimes call my friend Darby Conley (who draws *Get Fuzzy*) to talk about them. When I told him about this particular series (which I was pretty excited about), there was a prolonged silence. "A slaughterhouse? You're really gonna do a series of strips about a slaughterhouse?" "Yeah," I replied, "I think it's funny, until the end, when the girl Pig loves dies. She gets killed." That was followed by a *really* long silence. It's funny, but I sometimes have no concept of how dark my stuff can sound to other people.

Given that this pen only appears to be fenced on one side, I blame these pigs for not escaping.

71

I knew a girl in high school named Julene. My way of flattering old friends is to lend their name to a pig that is about to be turned into deli product. Odd they don't find that flattering.

You can say "gay" on the comics page, but it's a close call. Remember, in comics-land, the year is about 1955.

I will often hit my snooze button six or seven times in a row, raising the question of why I set the alarm so early in the first place.

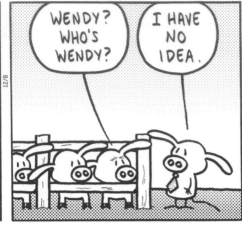

These are some of the lyrics to Bruce Springsteen's "Born to Run." I'm a big Springsteen fan.

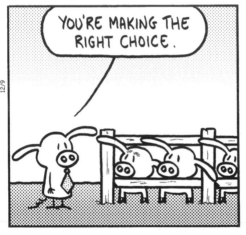

This is the closest any of these strips came to being an "animal rights" strip. I think I wrote it after reading the book *Fast Food Nation*, which exposes some of the ugly practices of the food industry.

PIG VISITS A SLAUGHTERHOUSE

OKAY, LULU...I GOT THE CAR STARTED! JUST HOP OVER THE FENCE AND WE'RE FREE!...FREE, LULU!

I'M NOT LULU... I'M JENNY.

THEN WHERE'S LULU?

SHE FLEW AWAY!

All right, all right, even I admit this one's a little over-the-top sad.

I HEARD YOUR FELLOW ZEBRAS HAVE ALL EQUIPPED THEMSELVES WITH MUSICAL ALARMS.

YEAH...WHEN THEY'RE CHASED BY LIONS, THE ALARM PLAYS CHRISTMAS CAROLS, AND WE ALL KNOW ONE OF OUR OWN IS IN TROUBLE.

THEN WHAT DO YOU DO?

WE SING ALONG.

I DIDN'T GET THAT E-MAIL YOU SAID YOU SENT TO ME YESTERDAY.

I RE-SENT THAT.

GET A LOAD OF MR. SENSITIVE.

This was one of my most popular Sundays. It's a rare one in that I generally rely heavily on dialogue, and this one tells the entire story with pictures. Also, I think the original last line was different. I think it originally said, "With a name like Mother Nature, you'd think she'd be a lot more kind." I changed it because I thought it was too wordy.

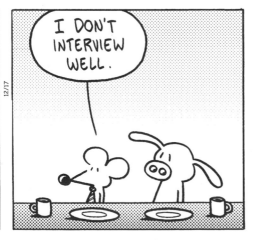

An honest interview would be very funny.

SIR, IF YOU'RE HIRED FOR THIS JOB, WHAT WILL BE YOUR GREATEST STRENGTH?

WELL...I THINK THAT ON MOST DAYS, I STEAL LESS THAN OTHER EMPLOYEES.

THAT'S YOUR <u>STRENGTH</u>? ...WHAT'S YOUR WEAKNESS?

ALL THOSE OTHER DAYS.

HOW'S YOUR SQUID?

SQUIRT

A LITTLE UNDERCOOKED.

This was a very old *Pearls* strip that first ran on the Web in 2001. In the original, the squid just stays on the plate. In this redrawn version, I thought it'd be funnier to have the squid actually leave.

I HEARD YOU CAUGHT RAT CHEATING AT "SCRABBLE."

YEAH... HE WAS STEALING EXTRA LETTERS THAT SPELLED BIG WORDS AND STUFFING THEM IN HIS CHEEKS TO HIDE THEM.

SO WHAT'D YOU DO?

I TOOK THE WORDS RIGHT OUT OF HIS MOUTH.

PEARLS
A Christmas
Tale

"...AND ON A SNOWY CHRISTMAS EVE, SANTA CALLED THE REINDEERS IN FOR A MEETING...."

BOYS, IT'S GONNA BE A TOUGH HAUL THIS YEAR. THE SLEIGH IS HEAVY AND THE SNOW IS THICK.

I HAVE FAITH IN YOU, SANTA. YOU'RE A GREAT, GREAT SLEIGH DRIVER.

WELL, THANK YOU, ROBBY... I APPRECIATE THAT.

OH, MY PLEASURE, SANTA... IN FACT, IT IS AN HONOR TO RIDE WITH YOU, SIR.

THAT'S VERY KIND OF YOU, ROBBY.

C'MON, EVERYONE...A BIG, BIG ROUND OF APPLAUSE FOR THE KINDEST, SMARTEST SANTA EVER.

"...AND LATER THAT EVENING, THE ANGRY REINDEER TIED UP THEIR SYCOPHANTIC BROTHER AND THREW HIM OFF A CLIFF......THE END."

POOR "ROBBY, THE BROWN-NOSE REINDEER."

I really liked this strip, and still do, but it didn't get a huge reaction. Maybe the word "sycophantic" threw people off. I should use simpler terms, like "kiss-ass."

Oh, boy. This series caused a stir. There were at least a couple cartoonists who were outright angry and let me know it.

Of all strips in the series, this is the one that caused the most controversy. The truth is that cartoonists have these debates all the time, but when you actually address these issues in the strip itself, it's a much bigger deal because you're taking the issues public. In retrospect, I'm glad I said what I did because I think a lot of it is true.

In the original of this strip, Rat mentions *Bloom County* as well, but then Berkeley Breathed came out of retirement, and the reference had to be deleted.

SO ARE THERE ANY OTHER REASONS THE FUNNIES AREN'T FUNNY?

SURE...UNLIKE IN ALL OTHER FORMS OF ENTERTAINMENT, THE CENSORSHIP CODE FOR COMICS REMAINS STUCK IN THE 1950's.

HOW DO YOU MEAN?

WELL, IN THE COMICS, YOU CAN'T MENTION THE SUBJECTS OF ██ OR ████ AND YOU CAN'T SAY THE WORDS "█████" OR "██████", DESPITE THE FACT THEY'RE SAID DAILY ON PRIME-TIME T.V.

GEE... THAT'S ████ED.

HEY, NOW.

12/25

This was a nice, warm, and fuzzy strip to run on Christmas Day. If I remember right, the "censored" words written on the original are (in order) "sex," "drugs," "sucks," "screwed," and well, I can't say that last word.

LOOKING AT THESE COMICS IS TOO DEPRESSING...I'M GOING OFF TO FIND GARY LARSON.

BUT I THOUGHT YOU SAID HE NO LONGER WANTED TO DRAW "THE FAR SIDE" BECAUSE—

OH, FORGET WHAT I SAID!!...THESE ARE DESPERATE TIMES! I'M SURE THAT IF I CAN JUST SIT DOWN AND TALK TO HIM FOR A FEW MINUTES, I CAN CONVINCE HIM TO COME BACK...

12/26

"...And what makes you think he lives here?"

I THOUGHT YOU WENT TO FIND GARY LARSON.

I COULDN'T GET BY HIS SECURITY COWS. I GUESS THE FUNNIES ARE JUST DOOMED.

WELL, I WAS THINKING...MAYBE WE COULD DO OUR OWN COMIC STRIP ABOUT THESE NAMELESS STICK-FIGURE ANIMALS WHO NEVER MOVE OR SHOW EXPRESSION, AND ALWAYS TALK ABOUT DEATH...

...I'D JUMP, BUT I'M AFRAID I'D CRUSH "DEAR ABBY."

12/27

I worried for weeks about this strip, and went back and forth with my editor at United as to whether we should ever run it. It was a huge departure from the general content of the strip. I even placed it at the end of December (just behind Christmas) on the assumption that not as many people would be reading the paper. I knew something big was about to happen when on Saturday (the day *before* it appeared), I started to get e-mail from people who buy their Sunday paper a day early. I never get e-mail on a Saturday for the next-day's Sunday strip. Even worse, the first few e-mails were scathing, all from angry pro-Palestinian people furious over the one-sided view the strip purportedly presents. I literally thought I had thrown my career away. I could barely sleep on Saturday night.

But the next day, the e-mail really started to pour in and, fortunately, those first few were not representative. Of the 2,500 e-mails I ended up receiving (far more than for any other strip I'd ever done), more than 90 percent were favorable. Of the letters that people wrote to newspaper editors, I'd say the ratio was closer to fifty-fifty, with the complaining half mostly upset about this topic being raised in what is supposed to be a humorous part of the paper. But more important, some of the e-mail I received was the most moving I'd ever read. A number of them were from the parents of Israeli children who had either died in such incidents or had come close to dying in such incidents, and their accounts were both shocking and heartbreaking. I had never had a strip impact people like this before, and it really showed me the power that one comic strip can have.

As it would turn out, December was the month of controversial strips (the slaughterhouse, criticizing the comics, the bus strip), and so, what better way to complete it than one more strip that would draw letters? And this was that strip. According to some newspaper editors who caught this before it ran, the word "fairy" is derogatory slang for someone who is gay. For me, it just meant "sissy." Due to this concern, the editors asked for an alternate strip using the word "sissy" (which we provided). As it turned out, some papers ran the "fairy" version and some ran the "sissy" alternate. The funny part here was that one paper on the West Coast caught the strip too late to run an alternate and chose instead to run blank space in place of *Pearls*. So that day, all of its readers saw a large hole in the middle of their comics.

84

These are a little harsh, but not nearly as harsh as the series that followed a year later, when I had Dickie the Cockroach put duct tape over Cathy's mouth and tie her up in a closet. Even worse, I revealed that when Cathy did not talk her strip was more popular with readers.

This was sort of a dumb joke, but people seemed to like it. Maybe it was the image of Barbie with shrimp on her head.

I hated that Magic Eye craze, mostly because I was never able to see the hidden picture. I'm convinced no one else could either, and that they all lied to me about it.

I think these are called "emoticons." They've got to be the most annoying thing ever put in an e-mail.

Rat's supposed to look a little bit like James Joyce in that first panel.

I WENT TO SAFARI BOB'S HOUSE TODAY.

IS THAT THE NEIGHBOR THAT HUNTS BIG GAME?

I DON'T KNOW. BUT I DO KNOW THAT WHILE I WAS THERE, A BUNCH OF ANIMALS STOPPED BY AND POKED THEIR HEADS THROUGH HIS DEN WALL.

YOU DUMB PIG...THOSE ARE ANIMALS HE'S SHOT.

YOU'D THINK THEY'D LEARN.

HI, SAFARI BOB...THIS IS MY PAL, RAT...HE WANTED TO SEE YOUR COLLECTION OF BIG GAME.

WHAT'S THAT IN YOUR HAND?

A CARROT...I BROUGHT IT FOR THE MOOSE.

PIG.... THAT MOOSE IS STUFFED.

WHAT'S ONE MORE CARROT?

I don't know why, but those big mustaches are always used as a visual cue for someone who hunts big game.

PIG IS GONNA BREAK INTO SAFARI BOB'S HOUSE AND FREE THE ANIMALS.

FREE THEM? THOSE ARE STUFFED ANIMAL HEADS.

HE THINKS THEY'RE LIVING ANIMALS WHO JUST POKED THEIR HEADS IN AND GOT STUCK, SO HE'S GONNA TRY AND PULL THEM OUT OF THE WALL.

OH, C'MON... YOU REALLY THINK HE'S THAT STUPID?

....FOLKS, AGAIN, IF I'M PULLING TOO HARD, YOU HAVE TO SAY SOMETHING.

It's probably bad form to say you like any of your strips, but I really loved this one. There's something so dark and wrong about putting a dead relative's head on someone's front porch and then fleeing.

In 2005 (over a year after this strip ran), the identity of the legendary Deep Throat was revealed, and unbelievably it turned out he had been living all these years in *my* hometown of Santa Rosa, California. Because I'm strange (and a big Nixon/Watergate history buff), I followed one of the many news vans that were here that day to his house and sat with the reporters on his front lawn. I even took a souvenir leaf.

Angry Bob was angry.
He went to the zoo.

Bob bought a pretzel and
a can of soda pop and sat
on a green bench facing
the monkey cage. The
hungry monkeys stared
at Bob.

"It is a good day for the
zoo," Bob thought. "It
is sunny and the pretzels
are warm and the soda
is refreshing."

"I am happy," Bob exclaimed. "I
thought I needed booze or new houses
to be happy, but I do not. All it took
was a warm pretzel and a refreshing
soda and a comfortable bench by the
monkey cage."

A projectile struck Bob in the ear.
A monkey screeched.
More projectiles followed.
Bob ran...

...straight into the path of
the zoo's biannual "Parade
O' Elephants."

Bob popped like a grape
and died.

DON'T TAUNT THE
MONKEYS.

Readers seemed to like this series.

I liked it, too, but if I had known how long it would take to draw those stupid refrigerator-magnet letters, I wouldn't have done it.

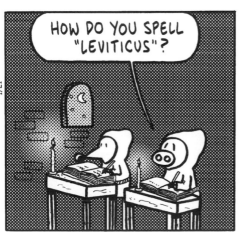

Rat's inability to see his own faults makes for easy humor.

Dear Mr. Rat,
I am in receipt of the next three chapters of your saga of Angry Bob, which you submitted to us for possible publication.

Please be advised that we here at the *New Yorker* have grown weary of publishing the mundane, lifeless prose of hacks such as John Updike, Joan Didion and Norman Mailer.

Why just this morning we thought to ourselves, "What we really need is something written by someone with a third-grade education discussing the perils of monkeys tossing their own excrement at zoo patrons."

1/25

Imagine our surprise when we opened your submission today and eyed your inspired work.

How reassuring it is to know that the future of western literature lies squarely in monkey \$#%@.

THANK YOU!
THANK YOU!
THANK YOU!

THE CHALLENGE NOW IS TO REMAIN HUMBLE.

I'm a big fan of all the writers mentioned in that second panel (Updike, Didion, and Mailer) and thought I'd try and get in a reference to them.

My dad once took me to a restaurant near his hometown of Phoenix, Arizona, and one of these bug zappers was right above the table where we ate. At least one fly's remains fell upon our table. Every time he recommends a new restaurant, I ask him if it's anything like the "bug zapper place."

The sign in the second panel is one you will probably never see in *Ziggy*.

This is directly out of my life. I worry incessantly right at the moment I'm trying to fall asleep.

I got to talk with Garry Trudeau just once, at a cartoonists' convention in Kansas City. I've always admired his ability to shake things up and withstand firestorms. Unfortunately, I had had too much to drink, and my opening line was, "Dude, you've got balls."

San Marino, California, is the town I grew up in. Louis is my cousin.

I wrote this after seeing someone knock on a watermelon at the grocery store. Like Pig, I'm not sure why people knock on watermelons. Unlike Pig, I'm fairly certain there aren't people living inside.

One time, I got to talk to Patrick McDonnell (the creator of *Mutts*) at the Schulz Museum in Santa Rosa, California. He mentioned that he got a kick out of this particular strip, which he said he had seen in his local paper. Maybe he was just being nice, but it meant a lot to me because I think Patrick's a great cartoonist.

In retrospect, I would have drawn this Rat-girl differently because I think her eyes make her look a little creepy.

I actually have a baseball autographed by Sandy Koufax and all of his Dodger teammates. I think I stole it from my dad—the same dad who took me to the "bug zapper place."

Rat's problem really is my problem. I'm terrible at showing empathy. When someone tells me their problems, I just try to offer solutions. For the life of me, I can't say, "Oh my gosh, that sounds terrible."

After this was printed, I heard from someone whose name really was Billy Kahn. After a few years of doing the strip, I've learned that if you give anyone in the strip a first and last name (which I generally do only when the name is going to be used in a pun), you're bound to hear from at least one person who has that name.

The Zeeba Zeeba Eata Fraternity of Crocodiles was not introduced into the strip until January 2005. But I had used various crocs in the strip well before that. This is one of those instances.

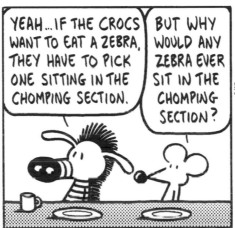

A number of people wanted me to do more of these Johnny-on-Top strips. I liked him, too, but my strip is not a political strip, and when I get even quasi-political, I always get complaints.

YOU STUPID PIG... WHAT DO YOU THINK—THAT THERE'S SOME SMILING GUY WITH A FLAG THAT SAYS "MR. HAPPINESS" WHO'S GONNA WHIZ BY ON HIS SCOOTER AND HAND OUT HAPPINESS TO ANYONE HE SEES??

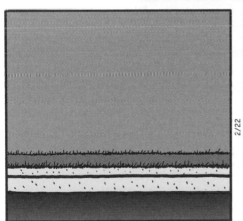

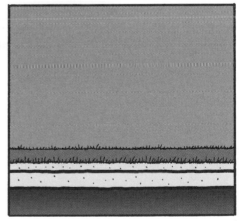

A lot of people seemed to like this one. Maybe on some level we can all relate.

After being so edgy (perhaps too edgy) in December, I decided to tone things down in February. Pig's sweetness is a good way to do that.

Of course, when I say "sweet," it doesn't mean I won't kill a family of small birds. "Sweet" is a relative term.

Dear Diary,
   I am still a caterpillar... I am beginning to think I will never become a butterfly.

Rat says this makes me a "self-loathing" caterpillar, which he says is no different than a "self-loathing" pig. But that's not true...

...I have more legs.

...SO THAT DUMB PIG IS DRESSED LIKE A CATERPILLAR, AND EVERY MORNING, HE GETS UP, RUNS TO THE MIRROR, AND CHECKS FOR BUTTERFLY WINGS.

HOW SAD.

YEAH. IT GOT SO PATHETIC THAT LAST NIGHT I TAPED LITTLE PAPER WINGS TO HIS BACK.

WOW. THAT'S THE FIRST KIND THING YOU'VE EVER DONE FOR THAT PIG.

I CAN FLY!

WHAT HAPPENED? WHY AM I IN THE HOSPITAL?

YOU GOT BANGED UP JUMPING OFF THE ROOF.

BUT HOW COULD THAT HAPPEN? I WAS A BUTTERFLY. BUTTERFLIES CAN FLY.

DUDE... YOU RAN SMACK INTO THE......

....

...MOON.

WOW...... the.... mooo........ .... ZZZZZZZZZZZZ

GET SOME SLEEP, YOU DUMB PIG.

A very rare strip, in which you actually see Rat caring about Pig. I'd do this more often but I don't want you to confuse *Pearls* with *For Better or For Worse*.

This is a strip where I wrote the first line, "The sea was filled with angry monkeys," and then sort of challenged myself to make something out of it. I was told later that this is more or less how improv comedy works.

It's funny: As long as you give Satan horns, the rest of him can be drawn any way you want.

Sure enough, as with Billy Kahn, I later heard from someone whose name was Thomas Good. I did not, however, hear from the Chin Brothers.

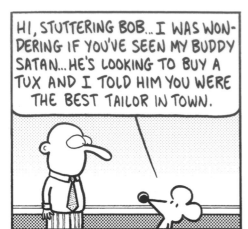

I want you all to know that Darby Conley (*Get Fuzzy*) thinks this is the worst strip I've ever drawn. In fact, he thinks it's so unbearably lame that when I bring it up, he starts laughing. Sometimes, when I think one of his strips is bad and he wants to know how bad, I'll say it's "da da tails bad," and we both instantly know that's code for "really bad."

I THINK THAT BEFORE WE'RE BORN, WE'RE IN SOME KIND OF PARADISE.

THEN WE'RE DROPPED DOWN HERE TO LIVE. BUT WE'RE USED TO PARADISE, SO THIS PLACE IS VERY PAINFUL.

TO EASE THE PAIN, WE'RE GIVEN TWO THINGS: MUSIC AND HUMOR. BUT OTHER THAN THAT, WE'RE ON OUR OWN.

ON OUR OWN... TO DEAL WITH THE LONELINESS AND THE TRAGEDY AND THE STUPIDITY.

YOU LEFT OUT CORNDOGS.

CORNDOGS?

CORNDOGS EASE THE PAIN.

3/7

...... I COULD USE A CORNDOG.

Once again, Rat's philosophy is my own.

This whole series was inspired by a *Speed Bump* cartoon that my friend Dave Coverly drew, where he had a dog owner about to hit a dog with a rolled-up newspaper and the dog says something like, "A newspaper? I'm not afraid of a newspaper. Look around you, Bob, we *live* in a newspaper."

I tried to smear the drawing with a newspaper to get this effect, but I don't think newspaper ink actually smears anymore, so I had to use a big thick pencil.

While I color all of my Sunday strips, I do not color the Monday through Saturday strips (the "dailies," as we call them). They are all in black and white. However, some newspapers like their dailies in color, and so they have them colored by a third party. This can occasionally cause problems, as it did with the color version of this strip, where someone filled in the entire TV with brown color. Thus, it ceased to be an incomplete TV outline and just looked like a full-blown brown TV, making the joke incomprehensible.

One *Pearls* fan cut this strip out and turned it into an actual refrigerator magnet, which I now have on my refrigerator.

116

The dumber the pun, the better.

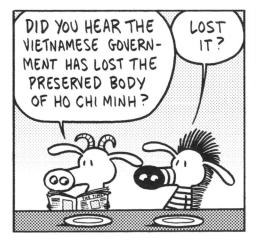

117

Darby Conley and my editor at United helped me rework this entire strip to tone down the impact of the word "Ho," which is being used here to mean a "loose woman." I can't remember the original strip, but I know the reworking was done so that a child reading it could legitimately think that the "Ho Chi Minh" mentioned in the first panel is the "Ho" mentioned in the second. The joke would then be ruined, but the child would not go running to his parents asking them what a "Ho" was.

On the original of this strip, the clown's name is "Humpy," but I thought that might be pushing it a bit.

Rat being me again. I've never actually broken the CD, but I've thought about it. Now that I just download everything from iTunes (where you can hear the music first), it's no longer a problem.

All I remember here is that that bar took way too long to draw.

This strip was supposed to be the beginning of a week of really bad puns, all involving this chicken. However, months after I had drawn them, I decided that I had been overdoing it with the puns and killed the rest of the week. (If you turn to "The Good, the Banned, and the Ugly" portion of this book, you can see them published there for the first time.)

I liked the concept of an overintrusive photo guy.

Well, I didn't say I'd stop doing *all* puns.

My favorite part about this strip is the third panel, where cartoonists appear to constitute their own gender.

Sadly, this really does represent my view of people.

This one would normally have been a Sunday strip, but I didn't think it was strong enough to justify a whole Sunday, so I compressed it into a daily.

As a kid, I listened to Steve Martin comedy albums over and over.

I gave this entire series to my accountant.

This was definitely my favorite strip in the series.

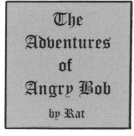
The Adventures of Angry Bob
by Rat

Angry Bob was sad.

"I do not want to be sad," thought Bob, "I want to be happy. I will start a parade."

Bob organized the "Toot for Joy" parade and handed out flyers and gave everyone kazoos and asked them to march in the parade and "toot for joy."

Bob even signed up a sponsor, the global fast food chain, Mickey Donalds.

On the day of the parade, a heavy rain fell. And no one came.

Except Bob, who stood in the middle of a downtown street, with his kazoo, and a shirt that said, "Toot for Joy - Brought to You by Mickey Donalds."

"I will not be sad," thought Bob. "I will toot for joy alone."

So Bob began to march. And as he turned the first corner, he saw heading toward him a different kind of parade....a parade of 100,000 angry people protesting the spread of large American global chains in the biggest anti-globalization rally ever organized.

And there was Bob, kazoo in mouth, wearing his shirt.

4/18

His Mickey Donalds shirt.

Enraged, the mob attacked Bob. With each blow upon his person, Bob exhaled, involuntarily blowing the kazoo and tooting for joy.

Many toots-for-joy later, Bob died.

HAPPINESS IS OVERRATED.

This was one of the most popular Angry Bob strips. I just like the image of Bob involuntarily blowing the kazoo every time he's punched.

I can't stand walking into stores and having commissioned sales guys jump me. I don't want to talk to anyone, particularly sales guys. It seems to happen the most in furniture and electronics stores.

I thought this was a funny series, but man did I get tired of drawing that same group of guys over and over. I resolved never again to write jokes that involve twelve or more guys.

I don't know about you, but in my experience, trying to get service done under warranty at these same stores is like reversing the polarity on a magnet: All those salespeople who rushed to you are now repelled by you.

These two dentists, Dr. Tripodes and Dr. Angelos, were named after my cousins. Both are dentists in Southern California.

I parody a lot of strips and rarely ask the creator of those strips what they think of them beforehand. But I know Patrick McDonnell and didn't want him to be upset, so I faxed these to him before they ran. He called me shortly after getting the fax and, unfortunately, didn't seem thrilled with the parody. (I'm just guessing, but maybe he didn't like the dark tone of some of the strips). Later, he called me back and said they were fine.

The character in the final panel is the father from *Baby Blues*.

This is the mother from *For Better or for Worse*, and Farley is a dog they had that died.

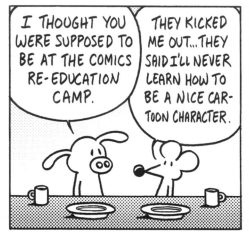

Of all the characters I drew this week, Bucky took the most time. I don't know how Darby draws that guy every day.

To be honest, I don't think I've ever even heard Yanni's music. He just seemed like a good guy to make fun of.

I actually go to bookstores and do this. And I'm always surprised that no one has ever asked for my ID.

Pig's statement in the second panel is all true. This entire week of strips had to be modified significantly. To see the strips in their original, unpublished form, turn to "The Good, the Banned, and the Ugly" section of this book.

*The only thing you will see up close is the inside of a frying pan, you big, fat succulent pig.

I always think it's funny when the reader knows something that the characters do not.

IN THE KIRCHUK PROVINCE OF KUKISTAN

* Klodski, you are back...Did you find good, cheap pork?
** Yes, I -- Holy Trotsky!...I lost him!

*Lost him? Didn't you explain to him when he jumped into the hole that he needed to slow down as soon as he saw daylight, or else he would risk blowing right through the other side of the earth?

** Please, woman...Even a stupid pig would know that.

NUTS.

I had some readers write to me and explain the actual physics of what would happen here. But I can't remember what they said.

WE GOT A PROBLEM, GOAT... PASTIS LAUNCHED PIG INTO ORBIT IN THE LAST STRIP, AND HE CAN'T THINK OF A CLEVER, LOGICAL WAY TO GET HIM BACK.

DON'T WORRY, RAT...PASTIS IS A SMART GUY... I'M SURE HE'LL FIGURE OUT SOMETHING CREATIVE INVOLVING SPACE TRAVEL OR ALIEN LIFE WHERE PIG GETS RETURNED TO EARTH IN SOME ELABORATE, INSIGHTFUL WAY.

AAAAAAAAHHHHH THUD!!

DID YOU HEAR SOMETHING?

142

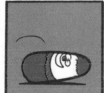

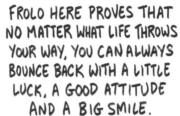

This is a good example of Rat and Pig's differing personas.

143

This was one of the most popular *Pearls* strips. After it ran, a number of people wrote to me to ask where they could buy their own "Mallets O' Understanding."

This was inspired by the Iraq debate and the question of whether it is ever right to preemptively invade another nation.

HOW CAN YOU SAY THAT? ARE YOU INSANE??

YOU'RE INSANE!! I REGRET EVER MARRYING YOU, YOU CHEAP, DUMB FAILURE!!!

LOOK FAMILIAR, FOLKS? YOU'RE OUT WITH FRIENDS WHEN SUDDENLY, YOU AND YOUR SIGNIFICANT OTHER GET IN A BIG, UGLY FIGHT RIGHT IN FRONT OF EVERYBODY..... TIRED OF THE EMBARRASSMENT?... WELL, NOW THERE'S HELP.

HI, I'M DR. RAT, AUTHOR OF THE BESTSELLING RELATIONSHIP ADVICE BOOK, "GIVE UP, WE'RE ALL DOOMED," HERE TO TELL YOU ABOUT AN EXCITING NEW ADVANCE IN MARITAL HARMONY WHICH WE CALL, "DISENGAGEOLOGY," THE SECRETS OF WHICH ARE AVAILABLE TO YOU NOW ON FOUR AUDIOCASSETTES FOR JUST $59.99.

5/23

AS 97% OF MARITAL FIGHTS BEGIN WITH CONVERSATION, WE'LL TEACH YOU HOW TO NEVER SPEAK TO YOUR SPOUSE AGAIN ... *YOU WON'T BELIEVE THE RESULTS!*

BUT THAT'S NOT ALL...BECAUSE SOME COMMUNICATION CAN BE DONE WITH FACIAL EXPRESSION, WE'LL PROVIDE YOU WITH SUNGLASSES AND A SURGICAL MASK, SO YOUR PARTNER CAN NEVER SEE YOUR EYES OR MOUTH AGAIN!

BUT WE'RE STILL NOT DONE! ORDER TODAY AND WE'LL THROW IN TWO LARGE 'HEFTY' BAGS FOR YOU TO SIT IN AND HIDE YOUR BODIES, TO PREVENT ANY SORT OF UNWANTED COMMUNICATION THROUGH BODY LANGUAGE.

ONCE YOU CEASE ALL VERBAL, FACIAL AND BODILY COMMUNICATION WITH YOUR SIGNIFICANT OTHER, YOU WILL NOTICE A DRAMATIC DROP IN THE NUMBER OF YOUR FIGHTS! ... AND SO WILL OTHERS!!

BOB AND SUE LOOK SO HAPPY TOGETHER NOW!

I'LL SAY!

ORDER NOW!

Wow. This one's *dark*. True, but dark.

The ultimate irony in my making fun of *Garfield* is that it is currently my son's favorite comic. As a result, I have purchased countless *Garfield* compilation books. Just thinking about it now is making me sad.

I probably use myself as a character in my strip more than any other cartoonist.

I don't know if it's true or not, but I once heard that the rock group Van Halen used to demand that all the red M&M's be removed from the M&M's bowls in their dressing room. Thus, Rat's demand in the second panel here.

WORSHIP THE RAT™

OKAY, RAT... YOU GOT WHAT YOU ASKED FOR. NOW PUT DOWN THE 'GARFIELD' BOOK AND UNLOCK THE PANEL.

OHH, NO...I'M NOT FINISHED, PASTIS. FROM NOW ON, YOU WILL DEPICT ME AS A ROMAN EMPEROR SURROUNDED BY HOT CHICKS WHO ARE FEEDING ME GRAPES. AND AHH, YES... I WILL SPEAK OF MYSELF ONLY IN THE THIRD PERSON.

ARE YOU KIDDING ME?

SHHHH...I AM TRYING TO SNEAK UP ON A SPIDER AND CRUSH HIM WITH MY ROLLED-UP NEWSPAPER. THIS, MY FRIEND, IS COMEDY!

5/27

YOU HAVE PLEASED THE RAT.

WORSHIP THE RAT™

OKAY, RAT...YOU'VE PUSHED YOUR LUCK TOO FAR. YOU'VE UTTERED SO MANY 'GARFIELD' PUNCHLINES THAT THE STRIP IS DAMAGED IRREVOCABLY. YOU HAVE NO MORE LEVERAGE TO USE ON ME.

RITA...BRING THE RAT A COPY OF "CATHY: A TWENTY-YEAR RETROSPECTIVE."

5/28

CLAP CLAP

I'M... GOING... TO KILL... YOU...

AAAAACK !! THE BATHING SUIT DOES NOT FIT !!

HAHAHA... THE RAT IS SO AMUSED.

Oh, my. Yet another cheap shot at *Cathy*. Have I no shame?

WHERE IS RAT TODAY? I THOUGHT HE HAD TAKEN THE STRIP HOSTAGE.

HE DID, BUT HE UTTERED SO MANY TRITE PUNCHLINES THAT THE COMIC POLICE BUSTED IN AND TOOK HIM AWAY.

WOW. I HAD NO IDEA YOU COULD BE IMPRISONED FOR TRITE COMIC PUNCHLINES.

YEAH. IT'S SCARY. I JUST HOPE HE'S NOT BEING HARASSED BY ONE OF THOSE PRISON GANGS.

5/29

... DIDJA HEAR THAT, GUYS ? THE RAT HERE THINKS HE DON'T HAFTA GIVE JEFFY HIS SMOKES.

The funny part about these parody series is that I usually run them in late May, when the National Cartoonists Society holds its annual convention. It's sort of a personal challenge to see if I can run these strips on the same days I'm going to be seeing these guys at a convention.

149

People seemed to like this strip. Pig's misunderstanding of common words makes for pretty easy jokes.

I don't think there were two people in the country who understood this. The sign, which you assume is supposed to say "Beware of dog," just says "Beware of do." The joke is that it's *supposed* to say, "do," as in "hairdo." The woman's husband is warning everyone about his wife's bad hair. I swear, it's funny. If only it could be understood.

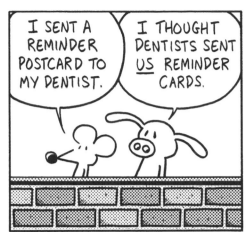

Like everyone, I can't stand going to the dentist. I hate getting lectured on the importance of flossing. Truth be known, I only floss the week before my appointment. I can say that here because I'm fairly certain my dentist will not be reading this book. If you know my dentist, please keep the book to yourself.

DEAR CROCODILES, LAST WEEK YOU KILLED MY BELOVED COUSIN, EDDIE ....

WHILE EDDIE MAY HAVE REPRESENTED JUST ONE MORE MEAL TO YOU, I WANT YOU TO KNOW THAT HE REPRE— SENTED MUCH MORE TO US.

YOU SEE, EDDIE WAS THE SMARTEST, MOST AMBITIOUS ZEBRA IN OUR HERD, AND WE HAD ALL HOPED THAT EDDIE WOULD GO TO A GOOD COLLEGE, AND GET A GOOD JOB AND MAKE ENOUGH MONEY TO MOVE THE HERD OUT OF THE PLAINS AND INTO A NICE CONDO.

BUT NO...YOU CHANGED ALL THAT. WITH ONE CARNIVOROUS INSTINCT, YOU WIPED OUT THE THOUS- ANDS OF HOURS WE SPENT HOLDING CAR WASHES, HAVING BAKE SALES AND SELLING BOXES OF COOKIES DOOR-TO-DOOR, ALL JUST TO RAISE MONEY FOR EDDIE'S FUTURE COLLEGE TUITION.

WHAT ARE YOU GOING TO DO TO MAKE UP FOR WHAT YOU'VE DONE??.... FOR KILLING OUR FUTURE PLANS?.... FOR KILLING OUR LAST HOPE ??....... TELL ME, YOU DESTRUCTIVE BEASTS!

6/6

DEAR ZEEBAS, WE BUY BOX O' COOKIES. NOW WE EVEN.

SIGH.......

152

This series arose from something I do at the Sunday breakfast table with my kids. I always make Mrs. Butterworth (who I call "Ms. Bootyworth") come alive. I make her voice real high-pitched and whiny, and have her beg the kids for mercy from "Evil Mom" (my wife), who insists on having pancakes and diminishing the syrup inside her. Ms. Bootyworth knows that once the syrup inside her is gone, she gets recycled and dies. Rather than showing any remorse to Ms. Bootyworth, my kids will often punch her (a punishment for her incessant whining, I believe). I then have the frustrated Ms. Bootyworth cry and run outside and stare at the kids from outside the kitchen window.

I didn't discover until a couple years into the strip how much more expressive Pig's ears can make him.

Looking back at these strips now, I notice that the crocodiles that appeared in *Pearls* prior to the Zeeba Zeeba Eata fraternity all had that same stupid accent even back then.

I thought it would be funny to have the love of Pig's life turn out to be a rather loose woman (or bottle, as the case may be).

Notice how the bottom of the soft drink container is tapered, so that it fits in the drink holder. It's the little details like that that make *Pearls* the visual masterpiece that it is.

I think this was inspired by the many *I Love Lucy* episodes I used to watch. When things went wrong for Lucy, they went very wrong, and all of her problems cascaded upon her at once.

The tragic demise of Ms. Bootyworth.

"Vinny" is another cousin of mine.

WELL, FOLKS, IT'S TIME ONCE AGAIN FOR THE 'PEARLS' MAILBAG, WHERE WE ANSWER SOME OF THE MANY E-MAILS THAT POUR IN EVERY WEEK HERE AT 'PEARLS, INC.'

OUR FIRST E-MAIL IS FROM CELIA L., OF SAN FRANCISCO, CA, WHO WRITES, "PIG IS SO CUTE AND KIND AND HUMBLE. HAS HIS SUDDEN POPULARITY CHANGED HIM AT ALL?"... WELL, CELIA, LET'S ASK PIG.

YO, GIRL, P. DIDDY PIGGY DON'T WANT NO PLAYAH HATAHS.

"Celia L." is a lawyer I used to work with at my law firm in San Francisco. I sent her the original of this strip.

THE 'PEARLS' MAILBAG

THIS 'PEARLS' READER WRITES, "IF I GAVE YOU $500, WOULD YOU NAME A CHARACTER IN THE STRIP AFTER ME?"

PLEASE, PEOPLE... AS MUCH AS WE'D LIKE TO ACCOMMODATE ALL FAN REQUESTS, WE ARE SIMPLY NOT GOING TO SACRIFICE THE INTEGRITY OF THE STRIP TO TURN A QUICK PROFIT.

ISN'T THAT RIGHT, THEODORE JAMES HAWKINS?

CALL ME TEDDY.

I get a lot of requests from readers to name a regular character after them. That's hard to do when your regular characters have names like "Rat," "Pig," "Goat," and "Zebra."

THE 'PEARLS' MAILBAG

OUR NEXT E-MAIL IS FROM STEPHEN H., OF BERKELEY, CA, WHO ASKS, "IS RAT AS RUDE IN REAL LIFE AS HE APPEARS TO BE IN THE COMIC STRIP?"

WELL, STEVE, PERHAPS YOU DON'T UNDERSTAND THAT I'M ONLY A DRAWING. WITH JUST A COUPLE SWIPES OF THE ERASER, I CEASE TO EXIST.

THIS CHANGES EVERYTHING....

"Stephen H." is another lawyer I used to work with at my law firm in San Francisco. My favorite thing to do with Steve was to wait until he went into one of the bathroom stalls and then throw three or four water-soaked paper towels over the top of the stall. The funniest part was that he was a partner in the firm and I was a lowly associate. I think you can see why I'm no longer a lawyer.

159

"I said, 'SMILE', Dolly Piggy.'"

I think I'd do a lot of things for $750,000 a year.

"Coverly" is Dave Coverly, creator of *Speed Bump*. He's not dead, though.

WHAT ARE YOU WATCHING, RAT?

IT'S A TRAVEL VIDEO ALL ABOUT SAN FRANCISCO... I'M THINKING ABOUT GOING THERE THIS FALL.

OHH, I *LOVE* SAN FRANCISCO... THE HILLS, THE CABLE CARS, LOMBARD STREET...

ME TOO... I WANT TO SEE FISHERMAN'S WHARF AND COIT TOWER AND CHINATOWN.

AND HOW 'BOUT THOSE GIANTS!

I *LOVE* THE GIANTS! DUDE, I AM THE WORLD'S <u>BIGGEST</u> BARRY BONDS FAN!

6/27

AND WHILE WE'RE THERE, LET'S BUY A COPY OF THE SAN FRANCISCO CHRONICLE... IT'S A *GREAT* PAPER!

A 'GREAT' PAPER? WHY, IT'S A *STUPENDOUS* PAPER!... WHY IT'S THE GREATEST, MOST STUPENDOUS PAPER SINCE—

GUYS... GUYS... WHAT ARE YOU DOING?

NOTHING.

NOTHING.

WELL, GOOD, BECAUSE I KNOW THAT THE SAN-FRANCISCO CHRONICLE JUST STARTED RUNNING 'PEARLS' AND I KNOW IT'S THE HOMETOWN PAPER OF THE STRIP'S CREATOR, STEPHAN PASTIS, AND A MORE CYNICALLY-MINDED PERSON MIGHT THINK THAT YOU'RE WILLING TO SACRIFICE ALL OF THE STRIP'S INTEGRITY IN A MISGUIDED ATTEMPT TO SUCK UP TO THE CHRONICLE AND THE ENTIRE BAY AREA...

THAT WOULD BE VERY CYNICAL.

GO NINERS.

I was so thrilled to finally be appearing in my hometown paper that I couldn't resist doing a little butt kissing. It was also a chance to plug my beloved Cal Bears (that's the pennant sticking out of Rat's bag).

A lot of people didn't get this strip. The joke is that Rat looks up at his profanity in the third panel and sees the planet Saturn (a common symbol used for swearing in the comics). He then gets it down for Pig to use in his solar system.

"Cretin" is a great underutilized word.

After this ran, I got a card from a whole bunch of people at PETA (People for the Ethical Treatment of Animals) praising the strip. I figure it will one day cancel out some angry complaint they'll send me.

Boy, did this one get letters. This time, the complaint was over the implication in the second panel that a bisexual *chooses* his or her sexuality. I just thought it was funny to use the word "desperasexual."

163

I CAN'T SLEEP.

PING PING PING

OH, SUPER...THE ANXIETEERS ARE BACK. WHAT'S IT TONIGHT, FELLAS?

IT'S YOUR GIRLFRIEND. SHE'S CHEATING ON YOU.

CHEATING ON ME?? WITH WHO?

KEN, THE GUY IN THE GRAPHICS DEPARTMENT.

KEN?

YEP. THE GUY SHE ALWAYS SAYS IS SO FUNNY...THE GUY SHE SAYS MAKES HER LAUGH.

...THE GUY SHE ALWAYS HAS "LUNCH" WITH.

7/4

THE GUY YOU MENTIONED YOU WERE SUSPICIOUS ABOUT, WHICH MADE HER YELL AT YOU AND CALL YOU "PARANOID" AND "OVERPOSSESSIVE."

NO NO NO NOOOOOO!! I CAN'T BELIEVE IT! HOW COULD SHE?? I...I...I..I .....

... I.......don't have a girlfriend.

WHAT?? ISN'T THIS 505 SANSOME STREET??

NO...IT'S 803 HEARST.

YOU IDIOT! HOW COULD YOU MESS UP?

FRED WROTE DOWN THE ADDRESS!

I DID NOT! BOB DID!

OHH, BLAME ME, WHY DON'T YOU?!

EVERYONE SHUT UP!! JUST SHUT UP!! WE'VE GOT TO GET TO 505 SANSOME FAST!

SORRY I'M LATE, HONEY.... KEN AND I HAD A MEETING.

OH.

I liked Alphonse, but he drew more complaints than any other character, all because of his threats to do himself in (see 7/7/04 strip below). When the topic of suicide is broached on the comics page, every suicide-prevention group in the country feels it's necessary to write their local paper and complain about what an unfunny topic it is. Personally, I thought the strips were funny. So there.

Rat reflecting my own paranoia again.

The funny thing is, I don't smoke. Why I always depict myself smoking is a bit of a mystery.

This series really had nothing to do with my characters, but by this point in the strip, I had learned that readers really hate it when your characters totally disappear for days at a time. So I had Pig attend the convention and tried to sneak him in as many of these strips as I could (even though he's not doing very much in most of them).

I'm proud of the smoke in that last panel. That's some well-drawn, quality smoke.

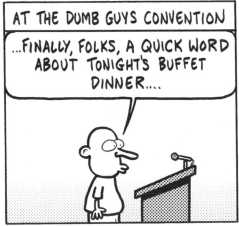

I'm the guy you hate in buffets that always messes up the salad bar. I try not to, but I drop crap all over the place. I'm sorry.

GEEZ, WILL YOU LOOK AT THIS? ACCORDING TO THESE SURVEYS BY THE NATIONAL CONSTITUTION CENTER, ONLY 41% OF AMERICAN TEENS CAN IDENTIFY THE THREE BRANCHES OF GOVERNMENT....

7/18

MORE THAN HALF OF ALL AMERICAN ADULTS DO NOT KNOW THE SENATE HAS 100 MEMBERS. ...AND ALMOST A QUARTER OF THIS COUNTRY CANNOT NAME A SINGLE RIGHT GUARANTEED BY THE FIRST AMENDMENT.

HEEEY, TAKE IT EASY, EINSTEIN....WHY DOES IT MATTER?

WHY?... I'LL TELL YOU WHY... BECAUSE WE LIVE IN A DEMOCRACY, AND THESE SAME PEOPLE WHO KNOW NOTHING ABOUT OUR GOVERNMENT <u>ELECT</u> THAT GOVERNMENT, WHICH MEANS THAT THEY DECIDE WHETHER OR NOT WE GO TO WAR, WHETHER CITIES ARE DESTROYED, WHETHER PEOPLE LOSE THEIR LIVES.

DUDE, YOU MADE ME MISS WRESTLING.

This stuff is all true (by "true," I mean I looked it up on the Internet and somebody said it, which is good enough for me).

170

I knew a guy once who figured out that his garage door opener also opened a neighbor's garage down the block. So whenever he drove by the guy's house, he opened the guy's garage door. Just for the heck of it. These are the kind of people I hang out with.

This confused some people. I'd explain it, but I don't understand it either.

I'm real big on these "(something) o' (something)" phrases ("mallet o' understanding," "box o' stupid people," etc.). When I look back on it, I think it's something I got from the early David Letterman shows. Letterman had a big impact on my sense of humor.

I almost always put those little apron/towel things around the waist of waiters. That way I don't have to draw the bottom of the coat, which I can't draw anyway. It's insight like that that makes your purchase of this treasury worthwhile.

This series reminds me of the "Fruit Buddies" series that's contained in the first *Pearls* treasury.

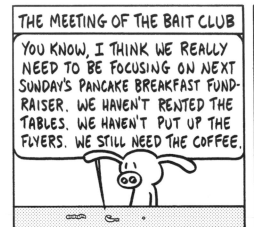

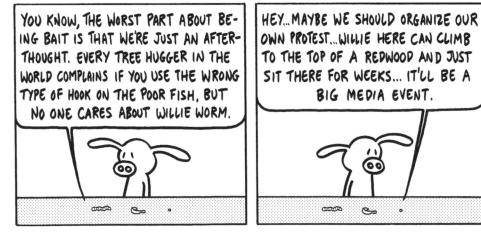

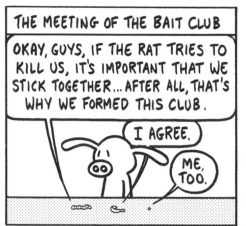

I don't know why, but every time I see Willie's line in that last panel ("Kill Sven now"), I laugh.

AUTHOR'S NOTE: It has come to my attention that virtually all "Pearls" series that are centered upon new, peripheral characters end in death. Whether it be the Fruit Buddies, Angry Bob or Tooty the Gingerbread Man, the newbies always die. As comedy is founded upon the unexpected, and death in these panels is all too expected, we now introduce a totally unexplored concept in "Pearls"... the happy, sappy ending. True "Pearls" diehards may wish to look away.

I'm frequently criticized for being too dark in the strip (Who? Me?), so this was my answer to that.

If you look real hard in the audience, you'll see Pig and a poorly drawn Dilbert.

When *Pearls* first began, I knew I needed a smart character in the strip. I decided it should be a bear (which looked pretty much like the one you see here). But when I showed it to my editors at United, they didn't like it. So I drew a whole bunch of different animals as possible replacements and let my editors pick the one they liked best. The one they picked was a goat. And thus Goat was born.

Man, this is straight out of my life. No hot woman has ever chosen to sit next to me on any flight anywhere. But how many times have I had the middle seat and had the two fattest men in North America sit on either side of me? It's too depressing to contemplate.

I've thought about doing this before. I've always wondered what the Realtor would do.

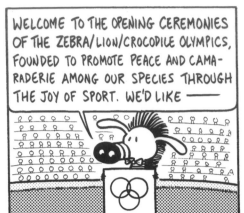

WELCOME TO THE OPENING CEREMONIES OF THE ZEBRA/LION/CROCODILE OLYMPICS, FOUNDED TO PROMOTE PEACE AND CAMARADERIE AMONG OUR SPECIES THROUGH THE JOY OF SPORT. WE'D LIKE ——

... WILL THE GROUP OF CROCODILES COOKING THE ZEBRA OVER THE OLYMPIC FLAME PLEASE STOP.

.... ROUGH START.

WELCOME TO THE OPENING OF THE ZEBRA/LION/CROC OLYMPICS... WE NOW GO DOWN TO THE FIELD FOR THE ZEBRAS' OPENING ADDRESS...

...WE ARE HONORED TO BE HERE TODAY WITH THESE OTHER SPECIES TO PROMOTE THE CAUSE OF PEACE AND BUILD THE BONDS OF BROTHERHOOD.

WHAT A BEAUTIFUL AND MOVING TRIBUTE, BOB.

YES, PETER, AND NOW FOR THE CROCODILES' OPENING ADDRESS....

CHOMP CHOMP CHOMP CHOMP CHOMP

... A MAN OF FEW WORDS, BOB.

YEEEES, PETER, HE KEPT IT SHORT.

WELCOME BACK, FOLKS, TO THE ZEBRA/LION/CROC OLYMPICS HERE IN ATHENS, GREECE...WE GO NOW TO BILL SIMMONS, WHO'S AT THE GYMNASTICS FACILITY FOR TODAY'S COMPETITION...HOW'S IT LOOKING, BILL?

NOT SO GOOD, BOB... WE'RE HAVING SOME TECHNICAL PROBLEMS HERE AT THE ARENA.

TECHNICAL PROBLEMS? WHAT KIND OF TECHNICAL PROBLEMS?

NO WALLS. NO ROOF.

TOMORROW.... WE DO TOMORROW... TODAY WE SMOKE.

YASOU!

I timed these strips to run at the same time as the Athens Olympics, because I thought for sure my fellow Greeks were going to screw something up (at the time, there were tons of construction delays and it looked like the main stadium wouldn't even be ready for the opening). As it turned out, everything went well, and that meant a lot of people probably didn't understand these strips.

WELCOME BACK, FOLKS, TO THE ZEBRA/LION/CROC OLYMPICS...TODAY'S EVENT IS SYNCHRONIZED SWIMMING, AND IT LOOKS LIKE OUR FIRST ZEBRA/CROC DUO ARE ALREADY IN THE POOL... HOW'S IT LOOKING, BOB?

YEEEES, PETER...THE PAIRING OF THESE TWO UNLIKELY SPECIES IS UNPRECEDENTED, AND REEEALLY SHOWS THE ENERGY AND SPIRIT THAT IS THE HALLMARK OF...........

AAAAAAAAHH!
CHOMP CHOMP
CHOMP CHOMP
CHOMP CHOMP
CHOMP CHOMP

......A HUNGRY CROCODILE?

THAT'S GONNA BE A BIIIIIG POINT DEDUCTION, PETER....

FOLKS, THIS JUST IN.....THE REMAINDER OF THE ZEBRA/LION/CROC OLYMPICS HAVE BEEN CANCELLED...THE OLYMPIC COMMITTEE CITED THE GREEKS' FAILURE TO PROTECT THE ZEBRAS AND THEIR FAILURE TO COMPLETE CONSTRUCTION OF THE FACILITIES.

THE GREEKS, FOR THEIR PART, HAVE DENIED THE ACCUSATIONS...WE GO NOW TO BILL SIMMONS, WHO'S AT THE TRACK AND FIELD FACILITIES WITH SOME OF THE ZEBRAS...UH....WELL, HE'S *SUPPOSED* TO BE WITH THE ZEBRAS... G#£# IT, BILL, WHERE ARE THE G#£#*G# ZEBRAS??

CRUSHED BY A BACKHOE, BOB.

WHERE HE COME FROM?

WHO CARE? TIME FOR COKE BREAK.

PEPSI! NO COKE!

That "Pepsi! No Coke" line is my homage to the Greek restaurant skit they used to do on *Saturday Night Live* in the 1970s.

WE HAD TO CANCEL THE ZEBRA/LION/CROC OLYMPICS... THE GREEKS WEREN'T READY AND THE CROCS KEPT KILLING US.

THAT'S THE WAY IT GOES, DUDE.

YEAH, BUT WHAT A WASTE... WE BOUGHT ALL THOSE MEDALS FOR NOTHING.

GIVE 'EM TO SOME LOSER WHO'LL APPRECIATE 'EM 'CAUSE HE'S TOO LAME TO WIN AWARDS ON HIS OWN.

NOT SO LOUD.

This idea came from a sign I saw at a beach in Bodega Bay, California. In my head, I just eliminated a couple of the letters on the sign and had a good strip for Pig.

Now that I look at it, that "lifting of the toilet seat" joke is more or less the same line I gave to the doomed piggy bank husband in the piggy bank series (earlier in this book). What is it with me and the lifting of toilet seats?

Here I am smoking again. And apparently, I now have a giganto-head. Well, at least I'm not making any toilet seat jokes.

This one is as autobiographical as they come. I'm always suggesting last-minute trips and it drives my wife insane. One good thing about being a syndicated cartoonist is that you can vent about your wife.

This was scheduled to run a couple times before this, but I kept pulling it because I thought it was too dark (it was the actual showing of the numerous zebra body parts that worried me). I finally ran it in late August, on the assumption that everyone vacations in late August and fewer people would see it.

Toby was way more popular than I ever anticipated. Scott Adams even wrote to me and said that this was the best week of *Pearls* strips I'd done to date.

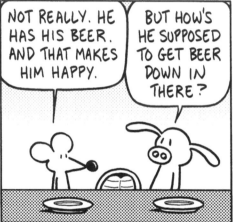

I'm certain that a number of editors saw the word "bong" and worried.

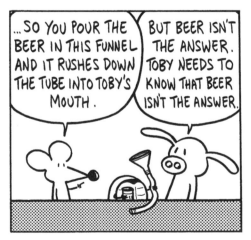

JUST BECAUSE TOBY THE AGORAPHOBIC TURTLE IS AFRAID OF PUBLIC PLACES IS NO REASON FOR HIM TO LIVE IN HIS SHELL AND GUZZLE FROM A BEER BONG.

...I THINK THAT LIFE IS BEAUTIFUL AND WONDERFUL ...AND MAYBE WITH HELP, TOBY CAN REALIZE THAT, TOO.

HIIYAA!!

POW!

TOBY REJECTS YOUR THEORY.

@#¢#¥&

GOAT, THIS IS MY FRIEND, TOBY THE AGORAPHOBIC TURTLE... HE FEARS PUBLIC PLACES, SO HE STAYS IN HIS SHELL AND DRINKS FROM A BEER BONG.

IT'S.... NICE... TO..... MEET...

POUR POUR POUR POUR
FOOOOOOOOSSHHH
GLUG GLUG GLUG GLUG
UUUUUUUURP

YOU.

NUTS. PASSED OUT AGAIN.

...HI, MR. PASTIS... PIG SAYS YOU CALLED.

YEAH... LISTEN, RAT... I FIRED YOUR PAL, TOBY, TODAY.....THERE'S JUST NO LICENSING POTENTIAL FOR AN AGORAPHOBIC TURTLE.

NO LICENSING POTENTIAL? HA! I KNEW YOU WERE A SELL-OUT, PASTIS! SO MUCH FOR YOUR BIG-TALKING "I'LL BE JUST LIKE BILL WATTERSON AND NEVER MASS-MARKET MY CHARACTERS" ACT! YOU HYPOCRITICAL WEASEL!

YOU'RE REALLY JUMPING TO CONCLUSIONS.

I wouldn't mind marketing Pig dolls. Maybe one day.

A PUBLIC SERVICE ANNOUNCE-MENT brought to you by **RAT**

HOWDY DO!

IT HAS COME TO MY ATTENTION THAT MILLIONS OF STUDENTS AROUND THIS COUNTRY ARE CHEATING IN THEIR ENGLISH COURSES BY SKIPPING THE ASSIGNED READING AND SPENDING HUNDREDS OF DOLLARS TO PURCHASE CANNED BOOK REPORTS ON THE INTERNET....

...THIS IS WRONG.

WHY IS IT WRONG? BECAUSE YOU'RE BEING OVERCHARGED. THAT'S RIGHT. SO YOUR FAVORITE RAT HAS TAKEN THE TIME TO READ THESE BOOKS AND PROVIDE TOP-NOTCH BOOK REPORTS TO YOU FOR THE ROCK-BOTTOM PRICE OF JUST $1.99 PER REPORT.

EACH OF THE COMPLETED BOOK REPORTS IS PRINTED BELOW. IF YOU LIKE THEM, SEND YOUR $1.99 TO RAT CO., CARE OF YOUR LOCAL PAPER.... THEN, JUST CUT THEM OUT AND TURN THEM IN. IT'S THAT EASY. NOW, WITHOUT FURTHER ADIEU, WE GIVE YOU.......THE REPORTS !

All Quiet on the Western Front

Big war.
Guy dies.

For Whom the Bell Tolls

Big war.
Guy dies.

The Great Gatsby

No war.
Guy dies anyway.

Death of a Salesman

Bad salesman.
Guy dies.

The Grapes of Wrath

Poor guy.
Guy lives.

8/29

JOIN US NEXT WEEK WHEN WE'LL TACKLE THOSE PESKY HISTORY BOOKS!

NOW....GO BACK TO YOUR NINTENDO™!

The funny thing is, I reread *Gatsby* and *Death of a Salesman* every couple years, and I'm a huge Hemingway fan. So I don't endorse Rat's shortcuts here. (See, we're not *always* alike.)

(Funny ending deleted at request of my syndicate.)

The truth is that I did have an ending for this strip, but I knew that there was no way I could ever do it, so I censored it myself and blamed the syndicate.

This was an easy joke, but I still liked it.

This was more or less a repeat of a strip I did in the first year of *Pearls* where Pig writes the same type of letter to Fidel Castro and makes Castro cry.

AND NOW, A PUBLIC SERVICE ANNOUNCE- MENT FROM YOUR FAVORITE RAT	KIDS, I DON'T KNOW ABOUT YOU, BUT FOR ME, THERE'S NOTHING WORSE THAN A TEACHER WHO MAKES YOU SLOG THROUGH BIG, FAT BOOKS ON AMERICAN HISTORY AND THEN FORCES YOU TO WRITE LAME REPORTS ABOUT EVENTS THAT HAVE NO RELEVANCE TO YOUR MTV UNIVERSE.	BUT NOW, THERE'S HOPE. YOUR FAVORITE RAT HAS READ THESE BOOKS AND DRAFTED INSIGHTFUL, CONCISE REPORTS ON EACH OF THE KEY EVENTS IN AMERICAN HISTORY. THESE REPORTS, WHICH ARE PRINTED IN FULL BELOW, ARE BEING OFFERED TO YOU FOR THE LOW, LOW PRICE OF $1.99 EACH.	SO, IF YOU LIKE THEM, SEND YOUR $1.99 TO RAT CO., C/O YOUR LOCAL PAPER. THEN, JUST CUT THEM OUT, TURN THEM IN, AND ENJOY ALL THE FREE TIME YOU'LL SAVE! SO, WITHOUT FURTHER DELAY, WE GIVE YOU RAT CO.'S TOP-NOTCH REPORTS.......

HIYA.

THE AMERICAN REVOLUTION	THE CIVIL WAR	THE GREAT DEPRESSION	WORLD WAR TWO	And now back to *Total Request Live.*
We don't like tea that comes from British people. So we kill them. Years later, we make up.	Guys with beards take their states and go home. We shoot them. Years later, they star in "Dukes of Hazzard."	Poor people from Oklahoma go to California to pick grapes. Those who stay in Oklahoma are immortalized in the Merle Haggard song, "Okies from Muskogee."	We save the French. They thank us by sitting in their cafes and smoking cigarettes.	 I WANT MY MTV!!

Like the Sunday strip the week before, this really doesn't reflect my own feelings. I love reading history books, particularly American history.

I remember being really depressed the week I drew these. Some people take pills for this. I draw giant beer cans attached to a rat.

For those who don't know, *Behind the Music* was a TV show that did these hour-long documentaries about famous rock stars. They seemed to really focus on those stars who had some horrible low point or tragic event happen in their careers.

This may be one of the only *Pearls* strips that involves Rat's mother. I don't think she's ever been shown, though. Rat's father was killed by a circus clown.

Toby was so popular that I brought him back for an encore.

193

9/13

SOMEWHERE IN ANTARCTICA.....

I had the hardest time drawing that penguin and those two guys in the last panel. No matter how many times I drew them, they looked like they were just resting on the ground. And if they didn't look flattened, there was no joke. Eventually, I got it right. Well, right enough.

9/14

POKE

9/15

WOW...YOU'RE DOING QUITE A BUSINESS TODAY.

SCORN $10

I WOULDN'T THINK THERE WAS SUCH A MARKET FOR SCORN.

THERE'S NOT.

SCORN $10

Acceptance (Free)

That's Dan Piraro (creator of *Bizarro*) about to be hugged next by Pig. Dan is one of the most all-around talented guys on the comics page.

WHAT THE ⑥✿₤# HAPPENED TO YOU, MORON?

I WENT TO A MAKEOVER SPECIALIST AND HE RECOMMENDED A HAIRPIECE. IS IT OBVIOUS?

DUDE, PLEASE, IT'S RIDICULOUS. NEVER LISTEN TO THAT GUY AGAIN. THE NEXT TIME YOU WANT TO CHANGE YOUR APPEARANCE, YOU ASK ME... GOT IT?

GOT IT.

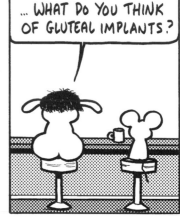

... WHAT DO YOU THINK OF GLUTEAL IMPLANTS?

GEE, MOM...WHY DO THE BABOONS HAVE THOSE BIG, PUFFY, REAR ENDS?

I DON'T KNOW, JIMMY...THAT'S JUST THE WAY GOD MADE THEM.

ZOO

AND WHY DO THEY LET THEM ROAM FREE AROUND THE ZOO?

I DON'T KNOW, JIMMY...I GUESS THEY'RE FRIENDLY... ...TRY PETTING ONE.

ZOO

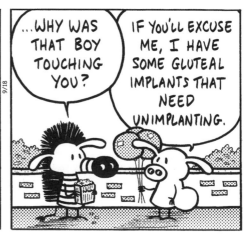

...WHY WAS THAT BOY TOUCHING YOU?

IF YOU'LL EXCUSE ME, I HAVE SOME GLUTEAL IMPLANTS THAT NEED UNIMPLANTING.

I didn't actually know why it was that onions made you cry, so I looked it up on the internet. Or, as George W. Bush says, "internets."

I'd have retyped that paragraph so you could see it more clearly, but I promised myself I'd never type that much text again. Suffice it to say that I made fun of a few cartoonists.

A lot of people seemed to like this one.

My friend has TiVo and swears by it. One day when he was at work and I had his condo to myself, I tried using it but couldn't figure the stupid thing out. All I kept hearing was this "bong" sound every time I pressed the wrong key. Eventually, I gave up and drank all the beer in his refrigerator.

I think it would be funny to fill your house with those store-bought frames and leave in the photos that came with them. When guests ask who the people in the photos are, you could make up tragic stories, or simply say, "I don't want to talk about it."

I did this strip right after hearing that Edvard Munch's *The Scream* had been stolen from a museum. More important, I think this is the only *Pearls* strip I've ever drawn while drunk. You can sort of tell from the lettering in the second panel.

This triggered a whole bunch of nice e-mail from women between the ages of forty and fifty-five who wanted to let me know that *they* liked my strip. The truth is I don't actually know the demographics of *Pearls* readers.

Looking back at this series, I just noticed that all the animals' names have repeated syllables ("Fifi," "Chi Chi," "Jojo," "Gigi," and "Pepe"). The odd thing is, I didn't do that on purpose. I guess I think those names sound funny.

201

This is my favorite strip in the series.

I was pretty shocked that I got away with this one. Believe it or not, saying "sex with your intern" on the comics page can cause problems. I think the fact that it ran on a Saturday (when perhaps less people read the paper) might have helped.

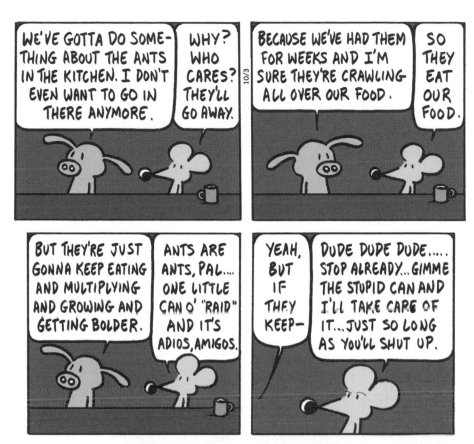

..."SHAKE CAN BEFORE USE... SPRAY DIRECTLY ON ANTS... KILLS ON CONTACT."... OKAY, ANTS, SAY HULLO TO MY LEETLE FREN—

Rat's line "Say hullo to my leetle frend" is a famous line uttered by Al Pacino in the movie *Scarface*. Embarrassing though it may be, I'd have to say that *Scarface* is one of my all-time favorite movies. I can quote a fair amount of dialogue from the film.

WHY WERE YOU LOOKING SO HARD AT MY TWENTY DOLLAR BILL?...

JUST WANT TO BE SURE IT'S NOT FUNNY MONEY.

HEEEEEY... I JUST FLEW IN FROM THE TREASURY DEPARTMENT AND BOY, ARE MY ARMS TIRED! BA DUM BUM KSSHHH... I'LL BE HERE ALL WEEK, FOLKS!

IT'S NOT.

HI, I'M PIG.... WAS THAT YOUR BOYFRIEND WHO JUST LEFT?

NO...HE'S NOT MY BOYFRIEND... WE'RE MORE LIKE "FRIENDS WITH BENEFITS."

WOW. I'D GIVE ANYTHING FOR GOOD HEALTH CARE INSURANCE.

WRONG BENEFITS.

OHH....DO YOU GET DENTAL?

PIG...I'D LIKE YOU TO SAY HELLO TO MY NEW SOCK PUPPET, PEPITO.

WELL, HELLO, PEPITO... IT'S A PLEASURE TO MEET YOU....

PUT THAT HAND AWAY, YOU BIG, FAT ©#Øf@⚡︎⚛︎©#≡ #☆*#☆ ©€§@ ☆§©# ♠€# ©✪*# ♠©✂︎♨ ♨♠€# OF LARD.

...WE'RE WORKING ON HIS SOCIAL SKILLS.

I like Pepito, but I'm not sure what inspired him. He's like a Muppet gone awry.

My spaghetti doesn't look much like spaghetti.

Any regular reader of *Pearls* knows from the first panel alone that Winky is doomed. No one named "Winky" is allowed to survive in *Pearls*.

This is based on personal experience. Anyone who's ever had any remodeling work done in their house knows what I'm talking about.

That object protruding from the bird's backside in the first panel is a tail.

Strip 1, Panel 1: ALPHONSE, THE NEEDY PORCUPINE, IS AT THE DOOR AND HE WANTS TO TALK TO YOU. HE SAYS THAT DUE TO THE UNCARING NATURE OF YOU AND OTHERS, HE'S GOING TO DO HIMSELF IN TONIGHT. THIS WILL BE HIS LAST DAY ON EARTH AND YOU WILL NEVER, EVER SEE HIM AGAIN.

Strip 1, Panel 2: PIPE DOWN, FATTY...'THE REAL WORLD PHILADELPHIA' IS ON AND IT'S TURNING OUT TO BE QUITE GOOD. I'D RANK IT SOMEWHERE BETWEEN THE SAN DIEGO SEASON AND THE LAS VEGAS SEASON. OF COURSE, NOTHING WILL EVER TOP THAT VEGAS SEASON. IT IS NOW LEGENDARY.

Strip 1, Panel 3: CAN YOU COME BACK TOMORROW?

I have to admit, I'm a huge fan of MTV's *Real World* and have been since the very beginning of the show. I love it.

Strip 2, Panel 1: HI, RAT... WHAT ARE YOU SELLING? / ADVICE... BUY SOME, BECAUSE I HAVE ALL THE ANSWERS.

Strip 2, Panel 2: OH, GOODIE... GIVE ME SOME ADVICE. / FINE. HERE IT IS...

Strip 2, Panel 3: DON'T TAKE ADVICE FROM GUYS WHO CLAIM TO HAVE ALL THE ANSWERS.

Strip 2, Panel 4: ... TIPS ARE WELCOME.

Strip 3, Panel 1: HELLO, RAT...THIS IS ALPHONSE, THE PORCUPINE. YOU'RE PROBABLY WONDERING WHY I HAVEN'T CALLED YOU TODAY. / I NEVER WONDERED THAT ONCE. I DON'T THINK ABOUT YOU.

Strip 3, Panel 2: THE REASON I DIDN'T CALL IS THAT I'VE TAKEN ALL MY BELONGINGS AND MOVED HERE TO HAWAII.

Strip 3, Panel 3: I MUST TELL YOU, THOUGH, THAT I WILL NOT BE PROVIDING YOU WITH A FORWARDING ADDRESS... I NEED SOME TIME TO BE ALONE...SOME TIME TO REFLECT UPON THE STATE OF OUR FRIENDSHIP... I KNOW THIS WON'T BE EASY...

Strip 3, Panel 4: ... BUT BELIEVE ME, I'M AS SCARED AS YOU. / SLUUUUURP

A rare scenic vista in *Pearls*. Please take note of the elaborate detail on those buildings.

I really do believe that people who obsess over their lawns are closet psychopaths.

I wanted this to be a series and have Rat work at a grocery store for the entire week, but at the time, I could only think of this one idea. Maybe I'll have him work there again one day.

A lot of people seemed to like this series. As a creator, I think this is definitely one of those instances where if you just think up the concept, the jokes will write themselves.

I've never bragged about how much I can bench, mostly because I can't bench very much.

That stupid cow took forever to draw. But I liked the strip.

I ran this series to coincide with the 2004 presidential election.

WELCOME TO "MEET THE PRESS."... I'M TIM RUSSERT AND I'M HERE WITH NEWLY DECLARED PRESIDENTIAL CANDIDATE, RAT... WELCOME TO THE SHOW.

GOOD TO BE HERE, TIM.

SIR... SOME OF YOUR CRITICS SAY YOU'RE A RIGHT-WING NUTBALL WHO'S EAGER TO INVADE ANY NATION THAT SO MUCH AS CRITICIZES THE U.S... HOW DO YOU RESPOND?

10/24

LIES, LIES AND MORE LIES, TIM... IN FACT, IF ELECTED, I WILL IMMEDIATELY WITHDRAW OUR TROOPS FROM BOTH IRAQ AND AFGHANISTAN.

SO YOU ARE AGAINST THOSE WARS?

WELL....NO, TIM... I'M ACTUALLY IN FAVOR OF THEM.

THEN WHY WOULD YOU PROPOSE WITHDRAWING THE TROOPS?

BECAUSE I'LL NEED THEM.

FOR WHAT?

TO INVADE THE LAND OF THE ARROGANT, EFFEMINATE, CHEESE-SNIFFING WEASELS YOU CALL "FRANCE."

...CARE FOR A "FREEDOM FRY"?

This didn't draw *one* complaint. For whatever reason, nobody ever sticks up for French people. They are the comedy equivalent of a "free pass."

Well, if nobody's gonna defend them, I'm just gonna keep taking cheap shots.

This was based on the infamous "Dean scream." I was watching Howard Dean's speech live at the time and I swear, my first thought was that the guy had torpedoed his whole campaign.

I have to admit, I've never actually read *Ulysses*.

RAT'S RUN FOR THE PRESIDENCY

SIR, IF ELECTED ON YOUR ANTI-FRANCE PLATFORM, WHAT ELSE WILL YOU TRY TO DO?

WELL, YOU'VE HEARD OF CHANGING "FRENCH FRIES" TO "FREEDOM FRIES" BUT I'LL EXPAND THAT TO OTHER THINGS.

SUCH AS WHAT, SIR?

WELL, LARRY BIRD WILL NOW BE FROM "FREEDOM" LICK, INDIANA... MR. FRENCH, THE BUTLER FROM "A FAMILY AFFAIR," WILL NOW BE "MR. FREEDOM," AND A KISS INVOLVING TONGUE WILL NOW BE....

LEMME GUESS... A "FREEDOM KISS," SIR?

YES... AND COULD C.N.N.'S PAULA ZAHN PLEASE COME TO THE FRONT FOR A DEMONSTRATION?

Shortly after this ran, I got an e-mail from someone on Paula Zahn's staff asking if Paula could have the original. I sent it to her. In exchange, she sent me a photo of herself, and at the top of it, she wrote, "To Rat . . . With Love and Kisses . . . Paula Zahn." It's sad when your characters get more action than you do.

WELCOME TO C.N.N.'S "NEWSNIGHT."... HERE'S YOUR HOST, AARON BROWN....

WELCOME, FOLKS...TONIGHT WE EXPLORE THE CURIOUS PRESIDENTIAL CANDIDACY OF RAT....

TO BEGIN, LET'S START WITH 'THE WHIP' AND OUR VERY OWN WOLF BLITZER, WHO'S STANDING BY WITH THE CANDIDATE IN WASHINGTON, D.C.

HAVE YOU BEEN A BAAAD BOY, WOLFIE?

...PERHAPS I MISUNDERSTOOD THE CONCEPT.

Wolf Blitzer did not ask me for the original. But hey, if you had to choose between hearing from Paula Zahn or Wolf Blitzer, who would you pick?

THE PRESIDENTIAL DEBATES

LISTEN, RAT, THIS IS A LIST OF FAMOUS LINES FROM PAST PRESIDENTIAL DEBATES...IF YOU GET IN TROUBLE, OR SAY SOMETHING DUMB, YOU MIGHT WANT TO USE ONE.

GOTCHA.

...MR. RAT... WHY SHOULD SOMEONE VOTE FOR YOU OVER SENATOR KERRY?

WELL... MR. KERRY'S FIRST NAME IS JOHN, AND A "JOHN" IS WHAT WE CALL A MAN WHO'S BEEN PICKED UP IN A PROSTITUTION STING...

WHERE'S THE BEEF??

For anyone who regularly reads the strip, Pig's dialogue in the fifth panel was a giveaway that it wasn't really him. I don't think he's ever called anyone a "moron" in the strip.

When we sent this strip to papers, we included an alternate strip that the papers could run instead (the alternate was just a repeat of an older *Pearls* strip). My fear was that there would be a fair number of editors who would not be comfortable with a strip praising fatal car crashes.

Of course, I had to follow up one offensive strip with another. So I thought I'd have Pig toss a baby.

This was the start of an experiment. I wanted to add a person to Rat and Pig's house who could serve as a permanent straight man for their jokes. But I needed a reason for him to live there. So I decided Rat and Pig would need him to help split the rent.

McGarry is named for my friend Steve McGarry, a great cartoonist and former president of the National Cartoonists Society. What better tribute than to make him a suicidal squirrel?

RAT SAYS THIS ACTOR CAN'T MAKE ANY MORE MOVIES BECAUSE HE'S UNDER SIX FEET.
HE'S SIX FEET UNDER.
THAT'S WHAT I SAID.
11/7
YOU SAID 'UNDER SIX FEET.'
IS THERE A DIFFERENCE?
THE FORMER IS DEAD.
HOW DID THE FARMER DIE?
FORMER.
HOW DID THE FORMER FARMER DIE?
FORGET IT.... ALL YOU NEED TO KNOW IS THAT THE LATTER IS TOO SHORT.
SO HE FELL OFF?
FELL OFF WHAT?
THE LADDER.
NO ONE FELL OFF ANY LADDER!!
...HE WAS...... PUSHED?
AAAAAUGHH!!
...I'D LIKE TO REPORT A SUSPICIOUS GOAT.

This was Leonard, the person I was going to add to the house. The character he plays at the park ("Tatulli, the Self-Esteem-Building Bear") is named after my good friend Mark Tatulli, who draws the strip *Heart of the City*.

Strangely enough, the last panel of this strip is one of the most painfully autobiographical panels I've drawn. I drew it immediately after my wife and I had a huge fight, all right in front of the kids. It made me feel terrible.

It's very easy to make fun of greeting cards.

Michael Jantze, the cartoonist behind *The Norm*, taught me one time how to mess with the print registration on my strip. So I used what he taught me to create this. The hardest part was making sure that no one tried to correct it before publication, because at first glance, it looks like an obvious print registration error.

AUTHOR'S NOTE: Due to the preceding story update, which was necessitated by the fact that "Pearls" continues to pick up new papers, the readers of which are not familiar with past storylines, there is no room left for a joke today. I asked the editors of many papers if I could borrow some space from "Mary Worth," but they said no.

I apologize for the inconvenience.

Yours,

Farina had not appeared in the strip for two years, forcing me to reintroduce her.

222

I think it's important to have at least one character out there who gets the better of Rat.

Round about this time, I realized that Leonard was a failed experiment. He wasn't a compelling character and I didn't like the way he looked. He also threw off the balance between Rat and Pig. So I decided I'd have to get rid of him.

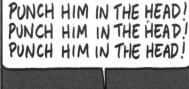

Poetry, particularly *angry* poetry, is very easy to make fun of. If you're a cartoonist and you ever run out of ideas, either throw in a monkey joke or make fun of poets.

For anyone who doesn't know, this is the mom and dad from the comic strip *Zits*.

And these are the parents from *FoxTrot*. I'm proud to say that I once had Bill Amend over at my house. He's very nice and as far as I could tell, he didn't steal any of the silverware.

I met Aaron McGruder only once, at the National Cartoonists Society's annual Reuben Awards in New York City in May 2000.

These are the characters from the comic strip *Luann*. We actually had to create a more innocuous alternate for this one, because we knew some papers were going to be uncomfortable with Luann's mom calling her new boyfriend "a young, hot stud." I ended up giving this strip to Greg Evans in exchange for a *Luann* original containing the hot vixen, Tiffany, which I specifically requested from Greg.

This character is from Pat Brady's *Rose is Rose* and was by far the hardest character to draw in this week of strips. Pat Brady is one of the nicest guys in all of cartooning.

THESE ARE MY TWO NEW PARAKEETS.... "ANAP" AND "PEEV."

I DIDN'T THINK YOU WANTED PETS.

WELL, YOU'RE WRONG....AND STOP EATING THAT DONUT.

WHY?

IT'S ONE OF MY PET PEEV'S.

SORRY..... I DIDN'T KNOW IT BOTHERED YOU.

IT DOESN'T BOTHER ME....YOU JUST SHOULDN'T EAT SOMETHING THAT'S NOT YOURS.

WHOSE IS IT?

I JUST TOLD YOU.

YOU JUST SAID IT WAS ONE OF YOUR PET PEEVES.

THAT'S RIGHT.

WHAT'S RIGHT?

THAT IT'S ONE OF MY PET PEEV'S.

AHHH!! I GIVE UP! MY BRAIN NEEDS A REST! I GOTTA GET OUT OF HERE AND TAKE A NAP!!

...HAVEN'T YOU CAUSED ENOUGH TROUBLE?

I showed these strips to Scott Adams before they ran, and he said he was fine with them. But I remember specifically that he didn't compliment any of them, so I've always secretly suspected that he didn't like them. The important point here is that this is how I treat the guy responsible for launching my entire comics career.

You will never again see me try to draw another bulldozer in *Pearls*. Much too much effort.

For those who don't know, part of the Elvis mythology is that he once shot a television.

I'm proud to say that I'm the only cartoonist to ever depict Scott Adams' butt crack in the comics.

A Message From Pearls Before Swine, Inc.

Dear Pearls Reader:

We interrupt today's scheduled strip to bring you this announcement.

Late last evening, we received a letter from the attorneys for Scott Adams, who has been featured in this week's series of strips.

The attorneys for Mr. Adams allege that Pearls has "falsely portrayed the Dilbert creator as a bizarre, obese, inarticulate and reclusive Elvis impersonator who sits behind the gates of his mansion shooting televisions, ripping his pants, and indulging in illegal narcotics."

The attorneys for Mr. Adams have asked that Stephan Pastis, the creator of the offending strips, issue an apology and a retraction.

In addition, the attorneys have demanded that the first two panels of today's strip be withheld from newspapers. According to the attorneys' letter, the panels in question took the Elvis analogy to "an inappropriate extreme" by "portraying Mr. Adams atop a toilet, whereupon he subsequently expired ignominiously of a drug overdose."

While the creator of Pearls will issue neither an apology nor a retraction, he has agreed to withhold publication of the first two panels.

We rejoin the strip in progress.

"Ignominiously" is another great underutilized word.

... THANK YOU ALL FOR COMING TO TODAY'S SÉANCE, WHERE WE WILL TRY TO REACH EACH OF YOUR DECEASED RELATIVES AND..... WAIT... WAIT.... I'M FEELING A PRESENCE ALREADY.....

12/5

GOOOOOAT... GOOOOOAT... IT'S GRANDPA...

GRANDPA ALBERT! GRANDPA ALBERT! HOW I'VE MISSED YOU!

HOLD ON.... I'M FEELING ANOTHER PRESENCE .....

ZEBRAAAA...ZEBRAAAAAAA......IT'S YOUR AUNT HILDIE.....

AUNTIE HILDIE? I CAN'T BELIEVE IT!!

HANG ON, FOLKS.... SOMEONE ELSE IS COMING IN...I FEEL IT... BUT WAIT.... IT SEEMS TO BE A.... A.... A......

..... SAUSAGE LINK ??

UNCLE GEORGE!!

WHO?

PIIIIG..... PIIIIIIG....

WHAT?

IT'S MY UNCLE GEORGE! HE WAS TAKEN TO THE PORK FACTORY LAST SPRING AND NEVER HEARD FROM AGAIN, BUT HE'S COME BACK TO TALK TO ME! WHAT JOY! WHAT RELIEF!... WHAT—

UUURP

... SORRY, DUDE... THOUGHT THIS MIGHT BE A BUFFET.

Personally, I thought this strip was very funny. I gave the original of it to my real-life Uncle George.

230

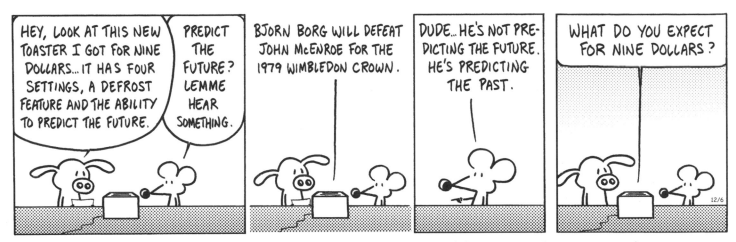

A number of people wrote to me to say that the toaster was wrong, and that it was John McEnroe who won Wimbledon in 1979. But I swear, I've Googled this about forty times now, and it says that Borg was the winner. And if the internet says it, it's true.

Hot on the heels of my alleged Borg mistake, a whole mess of people wrote to me to say that the toaster was wrong once again, and that the 1988 Summer Olympics were in Seoul. I was so angry at the people from the day before that I simply ignored all their e-mails. As it turned out, they were *right* this time. Oh, man, this was turning into one of those weeks.

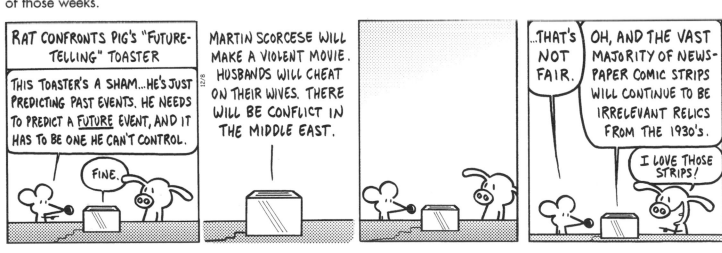

RAT CONFRONTS PIG'S "FUTURE-TELLING" TOASTER

THIS TOASTER CAN'T PREDICT ANYTHING... TAKE IT BACK TO THE STORE AND GET A REFUND. I WORK **HARD** FOR MY MONEY. I REFUSE TO BE RIPPED OFF.

CAN IT WAIT 'TIL TOMORROW? I TOLD SOME OF OUR NEIGHBORS ABOUT THE TOASTER'S PSYCHIC ABILITY AND THEY'RE PAYING ME SOME MONEY FOR A READING.......

12/9

PREPAAAAAARE TO BE AMAAAAAAAAZED.!!!

HAVE YOUR FUTURE TOLD! $25

THE TOASTER KNOWS!!

SEE THE INCREDIBLE TOASTRA-DAMUS!

HI, RAT... I JUST WANT YOU TO KNOW THAT I'M HAVING A "CELEBRATE ALPHONSE" POTLUCK DINNER NIGHT AT MY HOUSE ON TUESDAY... JUST A CHANCE FOR MY FRIENDS TO GATHER TOGETHER AND SHARE A LITTLE BIT ABOUT WHAT I MEAN TO THEM.

DUDE... YOU DON'T GET IT... YOU'RE A PATHETIC, NEEDY, OBLIVIOUS, DRAMA QUEEN LOSER... NOBODY LIKES YOU... GO AWAY... NEVER COME BACK.

12/10

CAN I PUT YOU DOWN FOR A JELLO RING?

I think this strip and the next strip marked Alphonse's last appearances in the comic. I just got so tired of suicide-prevention groups complaining to newspapers about the unfunniness of suicide that I gave up. A rare victory for my humorless foes.

HELLO, RAT... I JUST THOUGHT I'D LEAVE YOU WITH A FEW OF MY POSSESSIONS, AS I PLAN ON DOING MYSELF IN TONIGHT.

LISTEN, ALPHONSE, YOU CAN'T DO THAT.

OH MY GOODNESS! *YOU CARE!!*

YOU BET I CARE...

12/11

...I DON'T WANT THIS G#G# ON MY LAWN.

If you look really carefully, you can see that all of Alphonse's framed photos are of himself.

The moment I heard that the shrieking sounds played during the *Psycho* shower scene were actually from violins, I knew I had to do this strip with Pig. One of the cool parts about living where I live in northern California is that every time I go to the beach, I drive through the town where Hitchcock filmed *The Birds*. It's fun to see the locations from the movie.

WELL, HELLO, LISA... WHERE YOU OFF TO?

I'M GOING ON A SINGLES CRUISE...I'M HOPING TO MEET SOMEONE I CAN FINALLY SETTLE DOWN WITH...SOMEONE WHO ACCEPTS ME FOR WHO I AM.

WELL GOOD LUCK, 'CAUSE BOY OH BOY, YOU SURE HAVE A LOT OF BAGGAGE.

...THAT DIDN'T COME OUT RIGHT.

WHY'D THE CHICKEN CROSS THE ROAD?
Answer   1 Mile

TO GET TO THE OTHER SIDE

I SAW THAT JOKE COMING A MILE AWAY.

Sometimes people write to me to complain that they saw a certain pun in my strip coming from a mile away. So I thought it'd be fun to portray that literally.

SO IF WE PAY JUST $700 FOR A MILLION DOLLAR INSURANCE POLICY ON YOUR LIFE, AND YOU HAVE AN UNFORTUNATE "ACCIDENT," WE'D BE RICH....WE'D BE MILLIONAIRES.

YOU'D BE A MILLIONAIRE... I'D BE DEAD.

DO YOU HAVE TO PUT A NEGATIVE SPIN ON *EVERYTHING*?

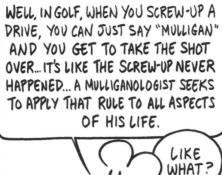

This was a popular strip. Goat's statement in the first panel is something I really do worry about.

Pig's sweetness is very important to the strip. Without it, Rat's bitter rudeness would be overwhelming.

Wee Bear was my attempt to create a Linus-type of character in my strip. I wanted somebody who was smart, goodhearted, and caring toward others. But I'm still not sure how well he fits into the strip and consequently, I haven't used him much since.

Another indication of my affinity for *The Real World*.

I once got to meet Robert Moses, and it was one of the most exciting moments in my life. Everyone's heard of Martin Luther King Jr. but few people today know what Moses did and how important he was to the civil rights movement. If you ever get a chance, you should read about him. He was courage personified.

Dear Rest of the world,
I hear you think we're nuts.

Well, it's not true...
Only some of us are nuts.

So I had an idea. We'll take our shortsighted, arrogant nutballs and send them to some island. You gather up your shortsighted, arrogant nutballs and do the same.

Once there, these cuckoo monkeys can strut and yell and throw coconuts at each other while the rest of us enjoy a nice cup of tea.

AWW... WHAT A NICE SENTIMENT TO SEND TO THE WORLD... IT'S SO BEAUTIFUL... DO YOU MIND IF I ADD A LITTLE SOMETHING?

OHH, YOU BET! THE MORE LOVE, THE BETTER... MAYBE THE WHOLE WORLD CAN COME TOGETHER AND SING AND DANCE.. AND... PLAY... AND....... AND...

12/26

OBEY.

MINOR TWEAK.

I'm with Pig on this one.

This is one of the very first series I ever did in *Pearls*, but I never thought it was very strong, so I kept delaying its publication. I finally ran it at the end of December 2004 (over three years after I drew it, I believe), on the assumption that not a lot of people read the paper in the week after Christmas.

240

This strip is sort of a tip-off to how old the series is. In the beginning of the strip, when I didn't know the characters well, Pig might have tried to one-up Rat like this. But it would never happen now, and thus looks totally out of character for Pig.

In going back and forth as to whether to even run this series, it was Rat's line in the last panel of this strip that eventually made me run it. I thought it was a funny line.

IT'S ABOUT A COCKROACH WITH NO TOLERANCE FOR STUPIDITY... IF YOU SAY SOMETHING STUPID, DICKIE TIES YOU UP AND SLAPS DUCT TAPE OVER YOUR MOUTH.

This and the next two Sunday strips were a big problem. In the originals of these strips, Dickie pulls off people's heads and puts the heads in his closet. But at the time these were first scheduled to run, news reports came in from Iraq of terrorists brutally decapitating their hostages. So we pulled the whole series and scheduled them for a much later date. But when this later date approached, these incidents in Iraq began occurring again, and so we pulled them a second time. When the third scheduled publication date rolled around, I decided there was no way they could ever run, so I substantially changed all three Sundays to the versions you see here. The originals of all three Sundays can be found in "The Good, the Banned, and the Ugly" section of this book.

This marked the introduction of the crocodiles as regular characters. I decided to move them into the neighborhood because I thought there'd be a lot more opportunities for jokes if Zebra and the crocs were face-to-face. Prior to this, Zebra generally had to write letters to contact his predators, and there were only so many letter-writing jokes I could do.

In the short time since they began appearing in *Pearls*, the crocodiles have become one of the most popular parts of the strip.

This is the continuation of the Dickie series I discussed earlier. After you look at the original, unmodified version of the strip in "The Good, the Banned, and the Ugly" section of this book, you can decide for yourself which version you like better.

245

Helloooooooo, new neighbor... Listen, we have keg party here at house tonight and we want invite you.... You good guy!

You're crocodiles.... If I came over to your house, you'd kill me and devour every last part of me... Now why would I come to a party like that?

HE MAKE GOOD POINT.

Hi, Mr. Zeba... My friend say you no come to crocodile party here at frat house tonight.... Maybe he no mention hot Zeba chicks that be here.

HOT ZEBRA CHICKS?

Ohh, what surprise!.... One here now!

Ohhhhhh... Me so lonely!.... Me so lonely!!

...Maybe he no like girls.

I get asked all the time what that accent is they speak. And the answer is that I really don't know. Their trademark opening line ("Hulloooo zeeba neighba . . . Leesten") sounds Russian to me, but I know that other people hear it differently. After that, it's just a hodgepodge. Mostly, they're meant to sound dumb, like Frankenstein or Tarzan.

LISTEN, PAL... I KNOW THE CROCS NEXT DOOR ARE TRYING TO EAT YOU, BUT THERE'S NOTHING WE POLICEMEN CAN DO ABOUT IT.

WHAT? THAT'S CRAZY... IF IT WERE A HUMAN THEY WERE TRYING TO EAT, YOU'D HAVE THEM DESTROYED.

YEP.... THAT'S THE FOOD CHAIN FOR YOU.

BUT THAT'S RIDICULOUS... IMAGINE THAT YOU'RE ME AND YOU'RE ABOUT TO BE EATEN BY SOME PREDATOR AND HURLED INTO THE GREAT BEYOND... WHAT WOULD YOU DO?

I'D COME BACK AS A HUMAN.

I think I've defied a few laws of physics in this last panel.

UPDATE

Last Sunday, Rat's comic strip creation, "Dickie the Cockroach," got loose in the Sunday funnies and slapped duct tape over the mouth of a very popular comic strip star.... We join the strip in progress.

This was the last strip in the series of Dickie Sundays that had to be modified. Again, the original, unmodified version of this can be seen in "The Good, the Banned, and the Ugly" section of this book.

HEY, THERE, RAT... I DIDN'T KNOW YOU LIKED THIS "ALL-YOU-CAN-EAT" BUFFET.

I DON'T. I HATE IT.

THEN WHY DO YOU HAVE ALL THAT FOOD?

'CAUSE I WENT TO THE SHOE STORE YESTERDAY AND USED ONE OF THE RESTAURANT'S PARKING SPACES AND THE ©#℮☾☆*@ HAD MY CAR TOWED... SO I'VE PAID THE $9.95 BUFFET PRICE AND NOW I'M GOING TO CLEAN THESE ©#℮☾*@ OUT.

NOW IF YOU'LL EXCUSE ME, I NEED TO HIT THE JOHN.

Shortly before doing this series, I went to a local "all-you-can-eat" buffet. On the wall was a sign that said patrons would be charged extra if they left uneaten food on the plate. I thought that was a bit draconian, so I vented my frustration by having Rat get into a fight with his local "all-you-can-eat" buffet.

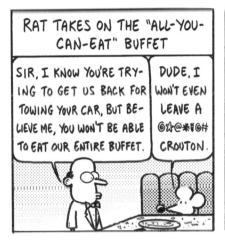

RAT TAKES ON THE "ALL-YOU-CAN-EAT" BUFFET

SIR, I KNOW YOU'RE TRYING TO GET US BACK FOR TOWING YOUR CAR, BUT BELIEVE ME, YOU WON'T BE ABLE TO EAT OUR ENTIRE BUFFET.

DUDE, I WON'T EVEN LEAVE A ©☆@*!©# CROUTON.

HOW 'BOUT WE JUST PAY YOUR IMPOUND FEE AND CALL IT EVEN?

HOW 'BOUT YOU MOVE YOUR #©☆ SO I CAN GO CLEAN OUT YOUR AU GRATIN POTATOES?!

FINE... IF THAT'S THE WAY YOU WANT IT!

YOU BET THAT'S THE WAY I WANT IT! AND THAT'S NOT ALL I WANT!!

OHH?! WHAT ELSE DO YOU WANT?!

A PUSH.

RAT TAKES ON THE "ALL-YOU-CAN-EAT" BUFFET

SIR, THE RAT'S CLEANED OUT THE ENTIRE BUFFET... THE SALAD BAR, THE ROAST BEEF, THE BAD PIZZA, THE MASHED POTATOES... EVERYTHING.

ALL YOU CAN E

I CAN'T BELIEVE HE DID ALL THIS JUST BECAUSE WE TOWED HIS CAR... HE'S DESTROYED THE RESTAURANT... HE'S GOTTA KNOW HE OVERREACTED, AND SOMEWHERE DEEP INSIDE, THAT'S GOTTA BOTHER HIM... I MEAN, WHAT ELSE CAN HE BE THINKING ABOUT RIGHT NOW?

MURRAY'S TUXEDOS?... YEAH, I THINK I'LL NEED A REFITTING...

RAT? WHERE ARE YOU?

I JUST LEFT THE DOC'S OFFICE. I GOT ME SOME OF THAT LIPOSUCTION.

WOW. DID IT GO OKAY?

WELL, SORT OF....THE MACHINE'S NOT REALLY EQUIPPED TO SUCK OUT 6,400 POUNDS IN ONE SITTING, SO IT MALFUNCTIONED A LITTLE, AND THEY HAD SOME TROUBLE SHUTTING IT DOWN.

YOU GONNA BE OKAY?

OH, YEAH... I CAN DO EVERYTHING I USED TO...

...EXCEPT WHEN THE WIND BLOWS.

1/20

PIG, THIS IS STEPHAN...LISTEN, I JUST WANT YOU TO KNOW I'M WRITING LEONARD OUT OF THE STRIP.

WHAT? THE GUY IN THE BEAR SUIT? HOW CAN YOU DO THAT?

BECAUSE THERE'S JUST NO LICENSING POTENTIAL FOR A CYNICAL DIVORCED GUY DRESSED IN A BEAR COSTUME.

BUT HOW YOU GONNA GET RID OF HIM?

I'M NOT SURE YET... I'M ACTUALLY A LITTLE BUSY RIGHT NOW, SO I ASKED RAT TO LOOK INTO SOME SCENARIOS THAT ARE FINAL, YET DIGNIFIED AND RESPECTFUL....I'M HOPING HE'LL COME THROUGH FOR ME.

1/21

LEONARD GOT HIS HEAD STUCK IN THE TOILET AND DROWNED.

PIG? PIG? ARE YOU THERE? PIG?

Long after I had made the decision to get rid of Leonard, I realized that I had never actually gotten rid of him. I had just sort of left him living there with Rat and Pig. So I decided to have him drown in the toilet.

I'M NERVOUS. I HAVE TO GIVE A SPEECH IN FRONT OF A LOT OF PEOPLE.

JUST REMEMBER... EVERYONE IN THAT AUDIENCE PUTS THEIR PANTS ON ONE LEG AT A TIME.

WHAT? THEY DON'T JUMP OFF THEIR BED AND TRY TO LAND BOTH FEET IN THE HOLES, MISSING OVER AND OVER UNTIL THEY BREAK BOTH ANKLES AND HAVE TO GO PANTLESS?

WHO DO YOU KNOW THAT DOES THAT?

1/22

...I'VE HEARD STORIES.

What better way to end this treasury than with the death of Rat? A true cliffhanger. Stay tuned.

The Good, the Banned, and the Ugly

The following seventeen strips are all strips that were either withdrawn or heavily edited prior to publication. In some cases, the content was considered too edgy or simply too likely to provoke complaints. The rest of them were pulled by me simply because I thought they were too dumb or too filled with puns. In any event, here they are now, in all their unedited glory.

This was the last strip in the Ho Chi Minh series you saw earlier in the book. Given the generous use of the word "ho" in the strip, my editors thought it would generate way too many complaints. Thus, it never ran.

The next five strips followed the chicken "coup" strip you saw earlier in the book. I nixed them because at the time, I thought I had been overdoing it with the puns. It's a hard to decision to kill strips, because each one represents a lot of work, but I think it was the right decision.

Holy smokes, this is a terrible strip. What was I thinking?

This one's passable, I suppose.

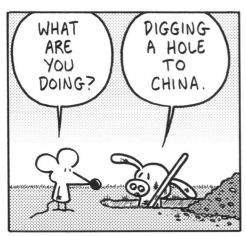

This and the next four strips are the original "Pig digging a hole" series. As you can see, Pig was originally digging a hole to China, but my editors thought that some people might find the series offensive. Thus, China became "Kukistan" and all the strips were edited.

* Tell me about it.

* I am Pin Li from the Shwang Duk province of China. I am looking for cheap pork to feed my large family. The fat one behind you looks delicious.

*The only thing you will see up close is the inside of a frying pan, you big, fat succulent pig.

IN THE SHWANG DUK PROVINCE OF CHINA

*Pin Li, you are back...Did you find good, cheap pork?

** Yes, I -- Holy Mao! I lost him!

*Lost him? Didn't you explain to him when he jumped into the hole that he needed to slow down as soon as he saw daylight, or else he would risk blowing right through the other side of the earth?

** Please, woman...Even a stupid pig would know that.

This strip provided the only small indication of what the original country was. If you look closely at my crude and incomplete globe, you can see that Pig is busting out of roughly where the same place China would be.

IT'S ABOUT A COCKROACH WITH NO TOLERANCE FOR STUPIDITY. IF YOU SAY SOMETHING STUPID, DICKIE PULLS OFF YOUR HEAD, TAKES IT HOME, AND PUTS IT IN HIS CLOSET.

This is the first of the original Dickie Sunday strips where Dickie pulled off his victim's heads. For the reasons stated earlier, all of these strips had to be changed substantially.

HEY, DID YOU MESS WITH THE 'DICKIE THE COCKROACH' COMIC STRIPS I DREW?

I DIDN'T EVEN KNOW YOU DREW A COMIC STRIP.

YEAH, IT'S ABOUT THIS COCKROACH WHO PULLS OFF THE HEAD OF PEOPLE WHO SAY STUPID THINGS...BUT SOMEONE ERASED DICKIE FROM ALL THE STRIPS I DREW.

HEY, MAYBE IT'S ONE OF THOSE FRANKENSTEIN-TYPE SITUATIONS WHERE YOUR CREATION CAME TO LIFE, ROSE OFF THE PAGE, AND MARCHED OFF TO TERRIFY THE VILLAGERS.

OH, MAN...WHAT A TRAGEDY THAT WOULD BE.

WHY DO YOU SAY THAT?

BECAUSE ME AND YOU LIVE ON THE REAL COMICS PAGE, AND THIS PLACE IS JUST FILLED WITH FOLKS WHO UTTER INANITY AFTER INANITY...IF DICKIE GOT LOOSE HERE, THERE'S NO TELLING WHAT HAVOC HE'D WREAK.

MS. GUISEWITE WILL NOT BE PLEASED.

This is the second of the original Dickie Sunday strips. I still think the image of Dickie carrying off Cathy's head looks pretty amusing.

UPDATE

Last Sunday, Rat's comic strip creation, "Dickie the Cockroach," got loose in the Sunday funnies and removed the head of a very popular comic strip star.....
We join the strip in progress.

The final Dickie strip.

This was another pun strip I killed when I was trying to decrease the number of puns in the strip.

This was just a bad strip. It's rare that I kill a strip for outright badness, but this one qualified. Please. Don't look.

I thought this one was a very funny strip, but I pulled it right before it was scheduled to run because I knew it would offend people. In its place, we offered papers a substitute strip. As it would turn out, one paper in the Midwest did not get the substitute in time and actually ran the strip you see above. And wouldn't you know it, a few weeks later I got two handwritten letters from readers of that paper saying what an offensive strip it was. I knew that if I got complaints from the readers of the only small paper that ran it, I would have been deluged in mail had it run everywhere. Ahh, the perils of doing an "edgy" strip.